PRAISE FOR

An Invitation to Celtic Wisdom

"This book inspires us to say 'yes' to life by giving us tastes of Celtic spiritual treasures. Carl McColman is a true shanachie—he loves telling stories that make our hearts sing."

—**Ray Simpson,** founding guardian of the
International Community of Aidan and Hilda,
www.aidanandhilda.org and author of
Daily Light from the Celtic Saints,
Celtic Christianity, and *Celtic Blessings*

"Franciscans recognize the headwaters of our own spiritual tradition in much of Celtic spirituality: nature based, optimistic, experiential, and much more mystical than moralistic. Carl McColman's stunning synthesis here is a great way to dive back into these wonder-filled and genuinely refreshing headwaters."

—**Fr. Richard Rohr, OFM,** founder of the
Center for Action and Contemplation

"With warm hospitality and the voice of a savvy storyteller, Carl McColman invites the reader to the feast of Celtic wisdom and prayer. In these pages, you will find a company of Celtic saints to walk with through our sacred landscapes, insights and good humor to guide you, and the clear voice of an author who knows the truth and depth of this tradition. Highly recommended."

—**Mary C. Earle**, author of
Celtic Christian Spirituality and
*Holy Companions: Spiritual Practices
from the Celtic Saints*

An Invitation to Celtic Wisdom

A Little Guide to Mystery, Spirit, and Compassion

Carl McColman

Broadleaf Books
Minneapolis

Cover design by Jim Warner
Cover photograph by Shutterstock
Interior by Timm Bryson, em em design, LLC
Typeset in Minion Pro

Print ISBN: 978-1-5064-8524-9
eBook ISBN: 978-1-5064-8579-9

Printed in the USA

For Phil Foster and Darrell Grizzle,
anamchairde
who walked with me between the worlds.

CONTENTS

TA mi lubadh mo ghlun
An şuil an Athar a chruthaich mi,
An suil an Mhic a cheannaich mi,
An suil an Spioraid a ghlanaich mi,
Le caird agus caoimh.
 Tre t'Aon Unga fein a Dhe,
Tabhair duinn tachar 'n ar teinn,
 Gaol De,
 Gradh De,
 Gair De,
 Gais De,
 Gras De,
 Sgath De,
 Is toil De,
Dheanamh air talamh nan Tre,
Mar to ainghlich is naoimhich
A toighe air neamh.
 Gach duar agus soillse,
 Gach la agus oidhche,
 Gach uair ann an caoimhe,
Thoir duinn do ghne.

I AM bending my knee
In the eye of the Father who created me,
In the eye of the Son who purchased me,
In the eye of the Spirit who cleansed me,
In friendship and affection.
 Through Thine own Anointed One, O God,
Bestow upon us fullness in our need,
 Love towards God,
 The affection of God,
 The smile of God,
 The wisdom of God,
 The grace of God,
 The fear of God,
 And the will of God
To do on the world of the Three,
As angels and saints
Do in heaven;
 Each shade and light,
 Each day and night,
 Each time in kindness,
Give Thou us Thy Spirit.

—From the *Carmina Gadelica*,
an anthology of Gaelic prayers from the
Scottish Hebrides, collected and translated by
Alexander Carmichael (1832–1912)

PART ONE

The Celtic
Mystery

A DHIA,
Ann mo ghniamh,
Ann mo bhriathar,
Ann mo mhiann,
Ann mo chiall,
Ann an riarachd mo chail,
Ann mo shuain,
Ann mo bhruail,
Ann mo chluain,
Ann mo smuain,
Ann mo chridh agus m'anam a ghnath,
Biodh an Oigh bheannaichte, Moire,
Agus Ogan geallaidh na glorach a tamh,
   O ann mo chridh agus m'anam a ghnath,
   Biodh an Oigh bheannaichte, Moire,
   Agus Ogan cubhraidh na glorach a tamh.

O God,
In my deeds,
In my words,
In my wishes,
In my reason,
And in the fulfilling of my desires,
In my sleep,
In my dreams,
In my repose,
In my thoughts,
In my heart and soul always,
May the blessed Virgin Mary,
And the promised Branch of Glory dwell,
   Oh! in my heart and soul always,
   May the blessed Virgin Mary,
   And the fragrant Branch of Glory dwell.

—*Carmina Gadelica*

Chapter One

The Mystery

The Celts are the people of the end of the world.

Visit the tip of the Cornwall peninsula and you will find a rocky placed called Land's End, where the thundering surf of the Atlantic pounds mercilessly against the ancient rocks. But once upon a time, it was Ireland—at least in the imagination of mainland Europeans—where you made your last stop before the vast, boundless ocean. The end of the world. All that lay beyond formed the stuff of myths and legends. A few hardy voyagers—we'll meet some of them in the pages to come—ventured out into the deep and came back with tales of lands like *Tír na nÓg*, the island of eternal youth, or the Land of Promise of the Saints, the closest place to heaven that could be found in all the earth. Aside from those heroic wanderers, for most people the west coast of Ireland, where the vast ocean continually pounded the shore, represented the edge of mystery, the gateway into an unknown and unseeable world.

Today we have lost that sense of the wondrous mystery awaiting us just beyond the edge of the ocean. A traveler leaving the British Isles heading west arrives not at *Tír na nÓg* or the Land of Promise, but rather comes to Boston or New York. So it may be difficult for us to appreciate that sense of openness to ever-present mystery that informed the poetry and stories and spirituality of the Celts long ago. We may know better than our ancestors, thanks to the round earth and the gift of flight, than to face the ocean fog with a sense of awe and wonder—let alone a wee bit of foreboding. But we make a mistake if we insist on approaching Celtic wisdom with a purely materialistic sense of things.

Perhaps the end of the world—the edge of mystery—is not so much a place on the map as it is a place in the heart.

Perhaps, even today, in our time hedged in by materialistic thinking and a culture besotted with entertainment and noise, we mortals are being invited into a spiritual "otherworld" as foreign and fearsome to us as the beach must have been to the first prehistoric creature who dared to crawl out of the ocean some half a billion years ago.

Since the Celts of old were so conscious of living at the end of the world, their wisdom and spirituality remain meaningful and useful for us, even today. Their way of seeing remains helpful to anyone today who seeks to enter the uncharted realms of mystery and Spirit. Great Britain and Ireland may no longer represent the ends of the physical earth, but they— or at least, the poets and saints, seers and wise ones who lived there—can still symbolize for us a final stopping place before that immense and mysterious journey to the mystical world that lies just beyond the reach of the senses.

To begin our journey into the mysteries of Celtic spirituality, we might begin by reflecting on the people of old whom we now call the Celts.

Are they simply the people of Ireland, Scotland, Wales, Cornwall, the Isle of Man, and Brittany (with Galicia thrown in for good measure)? For those are the lands, all situated on the western edge of Europe, that we now think of as the home of the Celts. But these folks actually represent the tiniest remnant of what once was a mighty culture, thundering across the continent in ancient times. We know from history that at the height of their worldly influence, the Celtic peoples called much of Europe home, from Ireland in the west to modern-day Turkey in the east. Galatia in Turkey, the place where a people called the Galatians received a letter from Saint Paul, was a homeland to some of the Celts. Perhaps when we read Paul's letter to the Galatians, we might think of it as Paul's letter to the Celts.

Another way to think about the Celtic world would be to include anyone who can trace his or her ancestry back to one of these lands. That adds millions, indeed hundreds of millions, of Americans, Canadians, Australians, New Zealanders, Patagonians, and various others into the mix. For that matter, may we suppose that the Celtic mystery enfolds everyone who comes to live in a Celtic land, or even anyone (of any ancestry or ethnicity) whose heart is stirred by the songs and poetry, the wisdom and spirituality of this ancient family of cultures and languages?

Each question leads to another. Just what makes the Celtic world "Celtic"? What separates Celt from Saxon or Roman or Slav? How is Celtic Christianity different from Roman Christianity or Greek Christianity or Syriac Christianity?

Such questions may shape a scholar's career or give a historian a sense of purpose and mission. But these are not the questions we need to be asking.

Celtic spirituality emerges from the heart of hospitality, of welcoming and invitation, of coming together. It's not particularly interested in what separates us from one another. The Celtic character is marked by kinship and convivial fellowship. It's a spirituality of stories and adventures, of conflicts fearlessly fought and love passionately shared. In other words, the Celtic people are a people of loyalty and relationship, characterized not by the ideas in their heads but by the fire in their hearts.

Language has a vital role to play in shaping the Celtic heart and mind. Celtic spirituality has its roots as much in language as in place. I have a shirt with a lovely saying in Irish on it: *Tir gan teanga, tir gan anam*—"A land without a tongue is a land without soul." There's a bit of politics in this, for the

Celtic languages for years were burdened by efforts of the English and the French to eradicate them, and today even if governments are no longer hostile to the ancient tongues, the indifferences of commerce and mass media continue to threaten the languages that once graced the lips of saints like Brigid of Kildare and David of Wales.

Language matters because each tongue carries not only its own vocabulary but also its own syntax—in its grammar, a language shapes the way its speakers view the world. This was beautifully conveyed in the science fiction movie *Arrival*, where aliens came to earth and brought a language that, as humans learned to speak it, sparked a revolution in consciousness. The question it begs: When languages such as Manx or Cornish disappear from the face of the earth, does a certain way of seeing the world, or even of knowing God, die with them?

I don't speak a Celtic language; I only know a smattering of Irish and Scots Gaelic. But I know enough to believe that these languages do in fact convey a way of seeing that is unique and vital, and even as the most basic of learners, I've received glimpses of that unique view. Perhaps it's not practical for us all to try to become fluent in the language our ancestors spoke, but I think we do owe it to them (and ourselves) to try to capture as much of their distinctive consciousness as we can, even given the limitations of our own tongue.

Speaking of politics, we can also say that Celtic spirituality represents the wisdom of a people who never were conquered by the Roman Empire, so they preserved an ancient way of seeing and knowing that was lost elsewhere. When the Celts embraced Christianity, they embraced a way of following Jesus that had not been compromised by the worldly power of the urban elites of Rome or Alexandria or Constantinople.

Living as they did on the very end of the world, the Celts forged an identity anchored in a deep sense of nature, a love of their land, a passion for kinship, and a love for the Spirit that embraced beauty and silence, solitude and self-forgetfulness, deep peace and deep listening.

How can we make Celtic wisdom our own? Especially for those of us who live far away from the islands on the edge, what does it mean to walk a Celtic path? It is a question that eludes an easy logical answer. The Celts are not so much philosophers as poets, not so much architects as artists. Their songs and lore invite us to discover meaning through myth and symbol and dream; to celebrate life through the crashing of wave on rocks or the whisper of a winter wind.

Perhaps the wisest way to walk this path is to immerse ourselves in the myths of the bards and the poetry of the saints, and consider how their lives illuminate our own. Indeed, no better way to embrace Celtic wisdom exists, at least as far as I can tell. But keep in mind that the stories are told in different ways, in different places and times. Keep in mind that you or I can hear the same stories or ponder the same legends and discern different rhythms in our heart and different paths on which we are called to walk. For the Celtic way is not shaped by sameness and standardization, but rather it celebrates the very kind of abundant diversity that makes the natural world so beautiful and so fearfully wonderful.

So let us tell the stories and sing the songs and enjoy the dance. Let us stand before the roar of the ancient ocean and climb the crags of the desolate high places. And most of all, let us listen to the silence between every beat of the drum that is our hearts. For in that silence we find something even deeper than a language that has been lost or a myth barely remembered. In the silence, we find our souls, and in our souls, we find the presence of God. For God is not elsewhere. God waits in the silence in our hearts.

Chapter Two

Three Streams

A Benedictine monk in Ireland suggested that there are "three streams" to Celtic spirituality.

Seán Ó Duinn was a monk of Glenstal Abbey in County Limerick. He was an expert on Irish history and Celtic spirituality, having written books on Saint Brigid and the folklore associated with the ancient megalithic sites of Ireland. Like a sleuth, this scholarly monk unraveled layers of stories, legends, and lore to shed light on the intricate web of relationships between the various ages of Irish spirituality. His understanding of Hibernian mysticism provides us with insight into the spirituality and wisdom of all the Celtic peoples.

First came the megalithic (stone age, or pre-Celtic) age, the age of the ancient sacred sites that still stand like mute sentinels on the windswept landscape: stone circles such as those found at Drombeg in Ireland or Callanish in Scotland; dolmens—standing stones that look like tables or altars but are actually the remnants of prehistoric tombs; and more elaborate grave sites such as Newgrange, a remarkable artificial mound oriented so that the sunrise of the winter solstice illuminates the tiny passageway into the central chamber where three tombs lay under an elaborate corbeled roof. Most of what we know of the beliefs and rituals of these ancient megalithic people comes to us through the silence of archaeological remains, although plenty of the folklore and myth that developed over the following ages speaks to the power and magic of these prehistoric sites.

Next came the Celtic age itself, an age of myth and poetry and stories, a time when warriors and druids shaped the destiny of the tribal peoples. We don't know exactly when the Celts first came to the lands now most associated with their identity: Ireland, Scotland, Wales, Cornwall, the Isle of Man, Brittany, and Galicia in Spain. There's even lively debate over whether the movement of Celtic culture into these lands came gradually and peaceably, or more suddenly as a result of invasion and conflict. The myths themselves embody the honor and dignity of a warrior people; indeed, the foundational text of Irish mythology is called the *Book of Invasions*. But regardless of how the Celts first arrived in their destined homelands, the tales recited by their bards—tales of gods and goddesses, champions and poets, sages and seers, druids and lovers—revealed the heart of their wisdom and spirituality, a magic that soon became synonymous with the lands where this distinctive culture took root.

The third stream represents the coming of Christianity. Once again, exactly how this happened may forever be shrouded in mystery. We have legends such as how Saint Patrick evangelized the Irish or how Saint Columcille brought the faith to Scotland; but the evidence beneath the popular legends remains sparse and contradictory, making the historical fact far from certain. Perhaps Patrick came to Ireland many years after an earlier missionary named Palladius, for example. Or were Palladius and Patrick contemporaries, or even two names of the same person? No one knows for sure. But we do know the Christians did come, and when they arrived, they stepped out from the confining safety of the Roman Empire to bring the message of Christ and his mercy and hope to a culture and a people radically unlike the familiar contours of "civilized" society.

When the Celts became Christian, they embraced new stories and new wisdom—the stories of Jesus and his apostles, as well as the emerging literature from the mystics of the deserts of Egypt and Palestine. But Celtic Christianity represented not so much the imposition of one religious identity on top of another, but rather the marriage or blending of the two. Christians brought with them tales of, and insights into, a God of mercy and forgiveness, incarnate in the healer and wonderworker from Nazareth; and the Celts responded by writing poetry that articulated their devotion, retreating into the wilderness to find remote places for prayer and sanctity, and—most surprising of all—preserving the ancient pagan lore of their ancestors in writing, something the druids themselves refused to do but the monks who followed Christ did with exuberance.

So, paradoxically, we have Christians to thank for the preservation of Celtic pagan lore.

These three streams of megalithic archaeology, pagan legend, and Christian lore combine together to give us the rich and heady waters of Celtic spirituality. It may not be the only kind of spirituality to emerge from the encounter between separate wisdom traditions—Christianity itself is the child of Jewish monotheism and Greco-Roman philosophy—but Celtic mysticism became a unique portal into the mysteries of the Spirit, a passageway that may be more essential and relevant—not just for Celts, but for all people—than ever.

What can we learn from such a messy history? If you want an exercise in frustration, go to your local university library and try to sort through articles and monographs by scholars who attempt to make sense of ancient Celtic spirituality. Many different theories exist as to how the Celts came to be, what exactly they believed, and why it matters (or doesn't matter) today. Meanwhile, every generation yields a new wave of romantics and dreamers who approach the Celts not with the steely logic of the scholar, but the playful lyricism of the visionary, which leads to new and different ways of entering the wonder and mystery of Celtic consciousness—but which also makes the possibility of understanding Celtic wisdom in any kind of logical way all the more elusive.

I believe it makes the most sense to approach the Celtic mysteries with a singing heart rather than an analytical mind. Celtic spirituality is the stuff of myth and legend. It is a story to tell, not a system to understand; a song to be sung rather than a proposition to be debated. If this way of thinking strikes you as fuzzy or lazy, I suspect you will find much of the literature of Celtic wisdom and spirituality to be more frustrating than enlightening. Even so, I invite you to keep reading, for one never knows when the whispers of eternity will break through even the most guarded, orderly mind.

When I gaze into the rushing and singing waters of the three streams, here's what I see:

First, I see that the stories we tell shape our identity. The ancient, prehistoric sites—from Newgrange to the stone circles to the old stone tables and the so-called fairy rings—all took on new life and new meaning when they were woven into the myths of the Celts. Newgrange became more than just an astronomically sophisticated burial place: it became the ancestral home of the gods who lived in the underworld. We can sanctimoniously dismiss the myths because they tell tales that "aren't true," but then we miss the insight into human nature or the mysteries of the psyche that are encoded within the signs and symbols of our legends and lore. C. S. Lewis is a helpful guide here: even though he regarded the Christian story as the only "true myth," he continued to draw from the wisdom and wit of many other legends and lore to celebrate their capacity to entertain us, and even more important, to teach us important truths about who we human beings really are.

In the three streams of Celtic spirituality, I see that the present and the past converse with one another, and perhaps with the future as well. When the megalith builders died out and were supplanted by the story-telling Celts, their land and ancient monuments spoke to the Celtic imagination—and that imagination, in turn, brought light to the Christian monks who sought to keep knowledge and wisdom alive during the so-called Dark Ages. What's beautiful about Celtic spirituality is how it brings these three streams of wisdom to us, here and now, calling us to embrace the insights of the past as a way to sculpt meaning and purpose for our lives at this moment—and to chart a direction for how we may live into *our* future with grace and compassion.

Finally, I notice that myth has a way of conveying truth and wisdom and insight that operate entirely outside the narrow ground rules of scientific thinking or modern scholarship. When I say this, I don't mean to dismiss the importance of empirical knowledge—so much of life today is enhanced and supported by technology and resources that come to us through our advanced science. But even the most carefully calibrated technical mind has its limits. Can science measure love or chart compassion or calculate a formula to resolve a finely nuanced ethical conundrum? Myth invites us into realms of wonder, of devotion, of sacrifice, of virtue, of paradox and mystery, of hope when all seems lost and compassion against all common sense. It snaps us out of the limitations of linear thinking into the creative possibilities of a future no one yet knows.

So Celtic spirituality makes us more complete as human beings. It does not compete with the empirical knowledge that shapes so much of modern life, but rather invites us into a wondrous otherworld where poetry and myth offer to shape us as well— and just as ordinary human knowledge teaches us the secrets of our physical universe, the "unknowing knowledge" of poetry and myth teach us the secrets of our souls, created as they are in the image and likeness of God. Celtic spirituality is not the only or exclusive portal into the realm of myth and wonder—but it is one such doorway, and one well worth exploring.

Chapter Three

Thin Places

One of the loveliest and most poetic expressions of Celtic wisdom consists of the idea of "Thin Places." Indeed, Thin Places can teach us much about spirituality in general, but also about the unique wisdom of Celtic mysticism in particular.

I discovered the notion of Thin Places the first time I visited Glendalough, the ancient monastery nestled in a glacial valley south of Dublin. We were there on a crisp October day, the forest filled with hardwoods dancing with autumn colors. Even as I stood in the carpark after first arriving, I could sense something special about the place; and when our tour guide explained that this was a Thin Place, my eyes sparkled with the gleam of recognition.

"Glendalough is a Thin Place," he said. "It's a sacred site, known to the Celts of ancient times, where the veil that separates our world from the otherworld, the world of silence and eternity, is particularly thin. So it's a place where we can sense the nearness of the eternal."

As I stood there at the edge of the forest, where it seemed that the memory of Saint Kevin and the other monks of Glendalough seemed especially present, I felt as if I knew, intuitively and deeply, just what he was talking about. And I recalled that I have known many such Thin Places over the years. I knew it the first time I visited places like Chalice Well in the shadow of Glastonbury Tor or the remarkable ancestral monument of Newgrange. I had sensed that Kildare, the home of Saint Brigid and several beautiful holy wells, brought me face-to-face with the unseen realm. And yes, I've had that similar sense of mystery and wonder at other places, both sacred and simple, I've visited over the years of my life.

Thin Places, all of them.

Not long ago I read a blog post by a woman who's unhappy with how people talk about Thin Places.

She pointed to Richard Rohr (among others) who speak of Thin Places as a particularly Celtic concept. She goes on to insist that Thin Places existed before the Celts ever arrived in places like Ireland, so of course it had to be *pre*-Celtic in origin!

Sigh. Even in the realm of Celtic spirituality, some people confuse the letter with the spirit.

Celtic wisdom makes sense because it points us to something true and universal, something deeply human and at one with the radiance of heaven. So it's a detour to get caught up on what is or isn't "really" Celtic, as if that were the final arbiter of what is good and true and beautiful. Yes, there is a character, a distinctiveness, to Celtic language and myth and story and culture, and it's good to celebrate what makes Celtic spirituality unique. But Thin Places matter not because they are Celtic (or pre-Celtic)—they matter because they are *real*, and point to something bigger than themselves.

The blogger's other point may be a bit more reasonable: that Thin Places really are *places*. In other words, it doesn't make sense to say "my heart is a thin place," or even to speak in generalized terms, like "the seashore is a thin place, because that's where I feel especially close to God." Well, I hope your heart (and my heart, and everyone's heart) *is* a place where we more readily touch eternity, and it's always lovely to hear about all the ways people feel especially close to the breath of heaven—and a beach or a garden or the mountains or the desert: all are locations that carry within them the seed to invite us into a place where eternity kisses us, fully on the lips.

But this begs a question. If just about every place could be a Thin Place, doesn't that render the concept itself rather, well—pardon the pun—*thin*? So I see the blogger's point: certain *specific* places truly are holy places, numinous places, places of sacrality—a college word that means "pertaining to the sacred." It's what theologians call "the scandal of particularity." It was originally applied to the Christian belief that Jesus is the one savior of all humankind—and even more than that, the one incarnation of the second person of the Trinity. Why would all people need just one particular savior? Because in a specific or particular expression of God's grace, the fullness of Divine Love is offered to *all* people. It's the idea of a *center*—every circle has a center, and you need the center to draw the circumference. Jesus of Nazareth, at least for Christians, is the center of God's saving love invading the universe and making all things possible. That's not to say that God's love doesn't erupt in countless other ways. Of course, it does. But for Christians, Jesus remains still the center of all the circles in our lives.

Thin Places work in a similar way. We encounter a particular "thinness" in places like Iona or Lindisfarne, Glendalough or Chartres. Out of these Thin Places, God's Spirit invades the world at large. Now when I say it doesn't make sense to call your heart a Thin Place, that's not to belittle the presence of God in your heart! Of course, your heart can also be a portal through which eternity flows into your life—I hope it is, and indeed I hope every heart functions this way. And every beach, and every garden, too, as well as every church.

But here is how I see the connection between Thin Places and the omnipresence of the Spirit (even to our hearts): perhaps we more easily recognize the inflow of the Spirit through our hearts or our gardens or our neighborhood churches because, even if just once or twice in a lifetime, we visit sacred sites like Chalice Well or Iona (or even a lesser-storied Thin Place in your own neck of the woods) where we find our hearts opened in a particular way—as if these places calibrate our spirits in such a way that we learn to recognize the whisper of the Holy, whenever or wherever it speaks to us.

Now I wish to speak of a few of the most renowned Thin Places, all of which have ties to some chapter of Celtic legend or lore. This is not an exhaustive list, by any sense. Think of it as an introduction to what is truly a vast topic.

I've already mentioned Glendalough, which literally means "the glen of the two lakes," located in the Wicklow Mountains south of Dublin. This is the site of a monastery associated with Saint Kevin (we'll be meeting him again in the pages to come). The ruins of the monastery still stand, with a lovely round tower, cemetery, and the lakes, carved out by glaciers long before the coming of humankind to Ireland. An ancient stone with a labyrinth also was found at this sacred site.

Skellig Michael, on the west coast of Ireland, became renowned after scenes for some of the *Star Wars* movies were filmed there, amidst the ancient beehive huts and rugged stairs climbing to the top of the mountain, jutting fiercely out of the windswept Atlantic. Today only birds like puffins and gannets live there, but once the island hosted Celtic monks, who retreated eighteen miles off the coast of Ireland to pray and chant in austere isolation. Some scholars think that, even before Skellig Michael became a Christian holy place, it had mythological meaning. Could it be the land of the eternally young, *Tír na nÓg*, where the Irish heroes and gods go after death?

Newgrange, on the River Boyne, is a massive structure built of earth, some 250 feet in diameter, with a lovely stone edifice and a small passageway that leads to three rooms deep inside it that served as tombs. Remarkable for its precise alignment with the winter solstice sunrise—on a clear day the sun shines into the heart of the monument for several minutes on the solstice dawn—the monument became associated with the fairies and gods of Celtic mythology, and continues to inspire visitors today with its silent witness to an ancient culture that honored its dead and revered the sun.

Chalice Well, located at the base of Glastonbury Tor in western England, is a holy site nestled in a lovely garden with a storied history. Legend suggests that the Holy Grail itself—the cup used by Jesus during the last supper—is buried or hidden deep within the well shaft, a charming bit of folklore bolstered by the high iron content of the water, which gives it a slight reddish tinge, mystically evoking the wine turned precious blood. The peaceful gardens today foster a sense of meditation for those pilgrims seeking not only the memory of King Arthur, but also legends that suggest Jesus as a boy came to the Celtic land of Cornwall with Joseph of Arimathea, a tin merchant who may have brought the lad as far inland as Glastonbury. But there are plenty of pagan associations as well, for this is also the ancient Isle of Avalon, mythically envisioned in Marion Zimmer Bradley's fantasy novel about priestesses of the goddess, *The Mists of Avalon*.

Kildare, the legendary home of Saint Brigid, is today a charming town about an hour southwest of Dublin, but a small cathedral and round tower testify to the site's original prominence within Irish Christianity. Once the home of a monastery where both monks and nuns lived and worshiped, today Kildare remembers its patron (or should we say "matron") saint with a festival on the eve of her feast day each winter, a spirituality center dedicated to her, and two holy wells within walking distance of the town center where people still pray for health and healing.

Tobernault, a holy well near County Sligo, is one of the most beautiful sacred sites in all of Ireland, famous from the days when Catholicism was illegal and priests would say mass there in the outdoors, far enough from town to evade the officious eye of the English authorities. Nestled beneath a cliff, the holy well remains a site of pilgrimage and prayer today.

Iona, off the coast of Scotland, is perhaps the most highly renowned of the great Celtic Thin Places. A small island in the Hebrides and the site of Saint Columcille's monastery, it is a legendary burial site for Scottish kings and today the home of the ecumenical Iona Community, which offers hospitality to pilgrims from around the world who seek to embody the best elements of Celtic Christianity in today's world.

These are just a few of the many Thin Places associated with Celtic spirituality. But if you don't live in England or Ireland or Scotland or Wales, that doesn't mean there are no Thin Places near you. They are there. You'll have to go looking for them. With your heart open and your soul keeping watch. Just pay attention, with your eyes and ears and, most important of all, your awareness attuned to the possibility that a particular place on the earth, a material point in space and time, can bring you to where you can begin to gaze into the limitlessness, the vastness, the timelessness of silence and eternity. Where the beating heart of Love beats with such urgency and presence that you could hear it, if only you were silent enough.

Such places of encounter are real. They are closer than you think. And as you get to know the wisdom of the Celts, it will make all the sense in the world why they were a people so capable of recognizing, and respecting, such places of openness and wonder.

Chapter Four

Holy Wells

In the preceding chapter I made several references to holy wells. From the Chalice Well in western England, to Tobernault in northwest Ireland, to countless wells throughout the Celtic lands dedicated to Saint Brigid or other much-loved saints—holy wells (water sources that serve as places of prayer and veneration) are icons of the Celtic spirit. I think I could say that every Celtic holy well I've ever visited is a Thin Place. So let's look at why this is so.

There is no "standard" holy well; they come in many forms. Some are wells in the traditional sense, where the locals have built round walls surrounding the water hole; a roped bucket hangs nearby, ready to help anyone quench his or her thirst. But many other kinds of water sources are venerated as holy wells. Many are springs, or even waterfalls that emerge from underground, and I've even seen one that is merely a crevice in a rock where rain water stands.

What they all share in common—and what separates them from ordinary or mundane water sources—is their sacred function as places where people go to pray, to worship, to intercede, and to seek healing.

Some holy wells are legendary for their healing properties. Many have particular reputations: one may be renowned for healing migraines, while another one nearby might be known for curing toothaches. Many Celtic wells are dedicated to a saint, often a local holy man or woman who may not even be recognized as an "official" saint by the church at large. Granted, most such wells are associated with renowned saints, especially Saint Mary and Saint Brigid. I don't know if anyone has done a particular study on holy wells, but my sense is that far more are dedicated to women saints than to men—but you will find the occasional holy well dedicated to male saints like Saint Patrick or Saint Colman.

People come to holy wells for the water, of course, treating it with the same respect that any pious Catholic would show to water from a shrine like Lourdes. Some holy wells even feature cups with signs encouraging visitors to take a drink. But there's more to your average holy well than just the water it yields.

In his poem "Little Gidding," T. S. Eliot talks about places "where prayer has been valid." In other words, a place where people routinely go to pray, like a cathedral or a sacred site associated with a saint or a miracle, over time begins to embody the energy of the generations of prayer made in that place, almost like it is a battery, fully charged with the energy of centuries of petitions and yearnings. This, it seems to me, is one of the secrets of holy wells: they are places where prayer has been valid, and they continue to attract us as special sites of spiritual power.

Often wells have "patterns" associated with them: formal procedures for praying at the well, usually involving the Rosary or other formal prayers and a particular route to walk while praying (for example, moving clockwise around the well nine times). Some wells even have signs that instruct first-time visitors how to properly follow the pattern at the well.

Many "accessories" to holy wells can be found at various sites. Some have human-made adornments: statues, gardens, walls, crosses, huts or shelters, all meant to give the well a sense of spiritual reverence as well as a feeling of being well cared for; indeed, many holy wells are located in beautifully tended grounds that function as a small park. Many wells are accompanied by a tree that has come to be venerated alongside the well; some of these trees are covered with *clooties*, small rags or strips of cloth that have been tied to the tree as a type of prayer remembrance. The legend of the clooties holds that they "carry" the prayers of the person who first tied them to the tree; as the clootie is slowly broken down by the elements over time, the prayers are "released"— almost like a time-released pill.

I must confess to feeling some ambivalence about clooties myself. While they clearly represent an ancient folk custom and are inspiring for the prayer and devotion they represent, on the other hand a tree covered by clooties could be hurt or even killed by all the tightly knotted strips of cloth. I'm not sure that God—or, for that matter, the ancient Celtic saints—truly require prayers to be made at the expense of an innocent tree.

Something else often found at holy wells: coins. Traditionally, the coins would have been tossed into the well, a custom that very likely has pre-Christian roots. Archaeology has shown that the ancient Celts would make offerings to their pagan gods by sacrificing valuable metal items to bodies of water. Entire hoards of votive offerings have been excavated from rivers, including swords, torques, shields, and other items fashioned from metals like silver or bronze or even gold. Although some of these items are clearly valuable from their composition of precious metals, scholars suspect that the armaments offered as sacrifices to the rivers were actually made for ritual purposes (a shield made of silver or gold likely was too valuable and not practical enough for use in a real battle). The ritual sacrifice of votive offerings leaves us with more questions than answers, but it suggests that the pre-Christian Celts saw water sources as sacred, and perhaps even as portals to the otherworld—the realm of the gods and the ancestors. By making offerings, the ancients were giving

gifts to their spiritual allies, hoping in turn for blessings, a fruitful harvest, or triumph in battle.

It's easy to see how the folk practice of tossing
a coin into a wishing well is a vestige of ancient
forms of sacrifice. This ritual has even extended to
fountains (the next time you visit a shopping mall
or an airport, stop and look at the fountains; they
will likely contain hundreds of pennies and nickels
and other coins, tossed in by passersby who were
making a wish or simply re-enacting an ancient
practice—or making a donation, since the own-
ers of many fountains now designate their "take"
to a worthy cause). Some holy wells even have coin
boxes installed next to the water source—which
may make good ecological sense, since throwing
the coins into the well could compromise the quality of the water.

Other wells, like St. Brigid's Well near Liscannor
in County Clare, Ireland, are renowned for various
other "sacrificial" objects left at the well: candles, ro-
saries, holy cards, or for that matter dolls, pictures of
loved ones, or even a pair of crutches. These votive
offerings symbolize the prayers of various persons
who visited the well.

One time I was leading a small group of American pilgrims through Ireland, and we stopped to pray at one of the holy wells near Kildare. While we were there, a local family came by to offer their own prayers, and one member of our group struck up a conversation with them. They were actually there to offer thanks; they had been praying at the well for their mother, who had been diagnosed with cancer, and they had recently received the good news that the cancer was in remission. So naturally they returned to the place of their intercession to offer a new prayer of gratitude.

I suppose some people might look at the folk practices associated with holy wells—tying ribbons to trees, executing precise actions while praying, treating the water with special reverence—and dismiss it all as only so much superstition. But I want to make the case for looking at holy wells not with the cold eyes of scientific skepticism, but rather the compassionate eyes that see value in tradition and myth and wonder.

Prayer is not magic, and traditional practices associated with prayer—like visiting a sacred water source—do not imbue the prayer with any more power than any other type of prayer might contain. So why go to all the fuss of visiting a well or following the pattern or treating the water with reverence? To answer that question, let's return to the idea of the Thin Place and how a particular action can help us remember a universal truth. We visit certain places because they seem to bring us face-to-face with the mystery of eternity. That mystery is always present in our lives—but we do not always pay attention to it.

We go to visit a place traditionally regarded as sacred, like a holy well, to help us pay attention. We perform the rituals associated with such a place—drinking the water, following the pattern, leaving a coin or some other votive object to symbolize our prayer—to help us remain mindful to a truth hidden deep within us. By joining in to long-standing folk customs associated with holy wells, we connect with people from generation after generation who have found comfort and inspiration by coming to these special places to pray and to praise.

What makes holy wells "Celtic"? The veneration of water sources can be found in many cultures around the world. But I think it's no accident that holy wells are so prominent in the Celtic lands. They are icons of the Celtic spirit, which means that in the veneration of holy wells we may find the gifts of Celtic wisdom: a recognition of God's presence in nature and the ordinary stuff of life, the importance of regular prayer, a sense that spirituality is not something reserved just for church or Sundays, but is intimately a part of everyday life. And since many holy wells do have associations with Celtic saints like Brigid or Patrick or Cuthbert, the wells reinforce the sense of communion and connection that living spiritual seekers today can find with the great Celtic saints of old.

Chapter Five

The Edge
of Waiting

Celtic Christianity is not a different kind of Christianity, as if Jesus had one message for the Celts and another message for everyone else. Rather, Celtic Christianity is a distinctive *expression* of Christianity. Let me offer an illustration of what I mean.

In Christianity, buildings dedicated to the worship of God are called churches—but also chapels or cathedrals or basilicas or shrines. Nowadays we have mega-churches, and from the beginning of Christian history, "house churches" have existed where believers gather in each other's homes.

Just as there are different types of churches, so too the buildings themselves come in all sorts of shapes and sizes. A modern mega-church might feel like a concert hall, a far cry from a medieval Gothic cathedral, with its flying buttresses, gargoyles, and intricately carved statues of saints. But as architecturally different as these structures might be, they serve a common purpose as a gathering place where Christians come to pray, worship, be spiritually educated and nurtured, and find inspiration to live in a more Christlike way.

So if all the various expressions of Christianity—Catholicism, Orthodoxy, Protestantism, Evangelicalism, and so forth—are like so many different types of churches, Celtic Christianity is like an outdoor chapel. Imagine a setting filled with the beauty of nature, where trees function as the pillars of the cathedral and the overarching sky serves as the ceiling, far above the grassy floor below. For the Celtic expression of Christianity, nature is the cathedral, the wilderness is the basilica, and a lovely garden is our neighborhood church.

It's not a different faith or a separate religion from all the other kinds of Christianity that have emerged over the past two millennia, but it is a singularly distinctive and beautiful *way* to respond to the love of God in Christ.

For just one example of how Celtic Christianity gives us such a uniquely beautiful approach to the faith of Jesus, let's look at prayer—specifically, contemplative prayer—through the lens of the Irish language.

The Irish word for contemplation—or contemplative prayer—is *rinnfheitheamh*. Yes, that's a mouthful! If you don't know Irish, even merely trying to say this word aloud can be an intimidating task. I have only enough Irish to be dangerous, and the pronunciation of Irish depends on which of several dialects you're speaking, but to the best of my knowledge, this word sounds like this: *RINN-eh-hev*.

So why such a big word for such a simple concept? Contemplative prayer, if you're not familiar with it, is a type of Christian meditation, a simple act of resting in silence before the mystery of God, a prayer of the heart rather than of the words and thoughts found in the mind.

Now, let's take *rinnfheitheamh* apart to appreciate the Celtic approach to contemplation.

Rinn means a "point" or a "tip," as in the sharp point of a sword. *Fheitheamh* means "waiting."

A literal translation of *rinnfheitheamh*, then, would be "at the edge of waiting"—which could easily be the most evocative and useful word for contemplation I've ever come across, in any language.

Remember, Celtic spirituality is the spirituality of the edge of the world. It's the spirituality that stands on windswept rocky shores, gazing westward to the open, stormy sea. It acknowledges that "edge" place in our hearts where time meets eternity, where words fade off into silence, and where heaven silently gazes into the turmoil of earthly life.

And we are always invited to gaze back, to gaze out of the chaos and the tensions and the paradoxes of our lives, into the silence, into the deep waters of eternity.

So to be a contemplative is to enter a place where prayer is shaped by waiting. This is not unique to the Irish or to the Celts. Indeed, waiting is a theme that crops up again and again in the Psalms. Jesus counseled his disciples to practice a spirituality of watchfulness, telling the story of the wise and foolish maidens as a cautionary tale about the importance of remaining mindful. Monks and nuns of the Christian mystical tradition, beginning with the hermits of the desert and carrying on through the Middle Ages, made a spirituality of attentiveness the anchor of all their days, waking before dawn to chant, to pray, to keep vigil, to keep watch, to wait.

Now, my other favorite word for contemplation is a Hebrew word for silence, found only four times in the Old Testament, and always in the Psalms. That word is *dûmiyyāh* (הַ֭רְמִיּה), which means not only silence but a kind of repose, a kind of *still waiting*. We find it in Psalm 62, in the line "For God alone, my soul in silence waits." Perhaps the most enlightening usage of the word is in the first verse of Psalm 65, in a verse that often gets mistranslated in English; the Hebrew literally reads "Silence is praise to you, O God on Zion, to you our vow must be fulfilled." But it's not any silence that functions as a way of worshipping God—it's the silence at the edge of waiting: the silence of contemplation.

The edge of contemplation is a sharp edge: an edge like the tip of a sword, the thin blade of the knife, an edge so sharp that it can effortlessly separate those things that need to be set apart. For a contemplative, this means setting apart the very words and daydreams and cluttery emotions that cloud our minds and hearts and distract us from the presence of God. When we pray at the edge of waiting, silence becomes a surgical scalpel to carefully remove our attachments to transitory pleasures or addictive compulsions. The silence of waiting sets us free—but it doesn't do so violently or instantaneously. That's where the "waiting" part comes in.

We pray at the edge of waiting when we bring our patience into the silence, trusting that the roots and thorns of our graspings and our anxieties must be slowly and gently pruned away, measured by a process of unraveling that opens us up according to the leisure of eternity, not the relentless ticking of terrestrial time. And yet, this waiting, this silence, this edge of prayer is something we live into breath by breath, heartbeat by heartbeat, instant by instant. The author of *The Cloud of Unknowing*, a medieval manual on the practice of contemplation, talks about the importance of remaining mindful through what he calls every "atom" of time, or "the least part of time" (we would probably say millisecond).*

Such unrelenting attention, of course, is virtually impossible to maintain; it seems to be part of the human condition that we remain easily distracted and prone to a mind wandering off in an infinite variety of directions (the author of *The Cloud of Unknowing* says that because of original sin, we cannot help but be easily distracted). But if we are committed to praying at the edge of waiting, opening our hearts and minds to the silence that comes to us from eternity, we are at least signaling to God that we are available to respond to God's call, whenever it may come. In the meantime, we wait, and we breathe into the silence that we glimpse between the words of our thoughts. And then we become distracted,

---

* There are units of time far smaller than milliseconds, including nanoseconds, picoseconds, femtoseconds, attoseconds, zeptoseconds, yoctoseconds, and the smallest unit of time anyone has been able to measure so far, the "Planck time." But considering that it takes a thousand milliseconds to equal one second, I suspect for most of us that's as small a unit of time that we need to worry about.

and then we return to attentively waiting. And such is the rhythm of contemplative prayer.

Sharp things are dangerous, so we might ask if the edge of contemplation has its own risks. Some have said that contemplation leaves us susceptible to the devil, but this is a misunderstanding. Temptation comes to us not through silence, but through words. So in a very real way, contemplation is one of the best safeguards against temptation. But the danger that we find at the edge of waiting comes in a more subtle way. We can fall prey to the idea that our unruly, distracted mind is somehow the enemy of contemplation; and that idea leads to a desire to, as one teacher of mine put it, "meditate aggressively." Aggressive meditation (or contemplation) happens when we try to force ourselves to be silent, when we try to beat away any random thoughts or distractions that interfere with our effort to be still before the mystery of God. Even *The Cloud of Unknowing* uses some unfortunate language about "beating down" any thoughts or ideas that come between us and the silence of God.

This temptation beguiles us to use the sharp edge of waiting not as a delicate scalpel, but as a broadsword, hacking away at anything we think stands in the way of our desire for being still and knowing God. But it's that temptation—which is, itself, a distracting thought—that wields the blade, and our intention to contemplate God soon collapses under the mistaken notion that we are "failures" at contemplation, simply because we are unable to find silence for much longer than a few graced moments here and there.

If we can set down the sword and be gentle with ourselves—in other words, return to the silence of waiting—then we soon discover that it is the Wild Goose who wields the scalpel (the Wild Goose is a Celtic symbol for the Holy Spirit). It is the Wild Goose who invites us with a whisper into a place of stability and rest where we discover that the sharp edge of our prayer never cuts away anything, but rather simply opens up a space within us where we can receive the loving gaze of God, beholding the One who beholds us, compassionately, joyfully, delightfully, eternally.

For this is the secret of *rinnfheitheamh*: we are always waiting, we are always shaped by longing for the One who can never be held but whom we may behold. But the waiting itself is a satisfaction; only it is a satisfaction that, paradoxically, deepens the longing. As we move deeper into silence, we realize that the silence is always within us, even if it is covered over by the noise of our restless minds. And realizing that the silence is always there, we discover that the edge of waiting is the center of our hearts.

PART TWO

The Celtic Saints

A RIGH na gile,	THOU King of the moon,
A Righ na greine,	Thou King of the sun,
A Righ na rinne,	Thou King of the planets,
A Righ na reula,	Thou King of the stars,
A Righ na cruinne,	Thou King of the globe,
A Righ na speura,	Thou King of the sky,
Is aluinn do ghnuis,	Oh! lovely Thy countenance,
A lub eibhinn.	Thou beauteous Beam.
Da lub shioda	Two loops of silk
Shios ri d'leasraich	Down by thy limbs,
Mhinich, chraicich;	Smooth-skinned;
Usgannan buidhe	Yellow jewels
Agus dolach	And a handful
As gach sath dhiubh	Out of every stock of them.

—*Carmina Gadelica*

Chapter Six

The Desert

To appreciate the uniquely Celtic expression of Christianity, it's helpful to consider the links between the earliest Celtic Christians—the renowned saints and wanderers who first brought the story of Christ to places like Scotland or Wales—and some of the earliest Christian spiritual masters, the holy women and men who lived as hermits and monks in the deserts of the Middle East.

In the Celtic lands, to this day many places have names like Dysart or Dysert. There's Dysart in Scotland, a suburb of Kirkcaldy, where a Celtic holy man named Saint Serf once lived. And there's Dysert O'Dea in County Clare, Ireland, the site of a monastery said to have been founded by Saint Tola in the eighth century.

Others can be found, sprinkled across the land, often with some sort of connection to a saint or monastery of old.

These names come from the Gaelic word *díseart*, which means "hermitage." It's an obvious cognate for the English word *desert*, which may seem a little odd, since the Celtic lands tend to be lush and green—Ireland is called the Emerald Isle, not the Sandy Isle.

Although some places in the Celtic world truly are austere and desolate—for example, the windswept islands of the Hebrides or the Skelligs, or the limestone-covered Burren in the west of Ireland, which looks like a moonscape here on earth—*desert* is not really a word that leaps to mind when we think of the lands where the Celtic saints lived.

So what's the story behind these *díseart* place names? There are those who say it goes back to the earliest days of Celtic Christian spirituality—the spirituality that inspired the great saints like Patrick and Brigid and Columcille. In trying to see the link between the desert and the first Celtic Christians, perhaps we will find a clue to understanding the roots of Celtic Christianity, roots that help us to see how Celtic wisdom fits in with Christian spirituality as a whole.

To begin with, deserts have been part of the Christian story since, well, the life of Jesus himself. After Jesus was baptized, the Bible tells us that the Holy Spirit drove him into the wilderness—the desert—where he lived like a hermit, fasting for forty days and forty nights. This led to an otherworldly encounter with the spirit of evil, who proceeded to tempt Jesus in several ways. The evil one encouraged Jesus to assuage his hunger by performing miracles—turning stone to bread. Then he tried to goad Jesus into proving his spiritual mastery, by throwing himself off a parapet of the temple, trusting the angels to save him. Finally, the tempter offered what can truly be called a devil's bargain: in exchange for worshipping the evil one, Jesus would receive earthly power and renown.

Jesus, naturally, rejected all these temptations and went on to begin his ministry of healing and teaching that would culminate a few years later in his passion, death, and resurrection. But ever since the story of his desert sojourn and temptation in the wilderness was recorded in the New Testament, it has fired the imagination of each succeeding generation of Christian spiritual seekers.

By the third century, desert and wilderness settings across Egypt, Palestine, and Syria had become a destination for people who wanted to give everything to God. By the early fourth century, Christianity was no longer an illegal religion in the Roman world, which meant that the most extreme way a person could express his or her faith—by being martyred for the cause—was no longer going to happen. Perhaps most Christians simply breathed a sigh of relief at this turn of events. But there were some who wanted no limit to their devotion: they wanted to give themselves as fully as they could to the path of following Christ. Once Christians were no longer persecuted by the civil authorities, withdrawing into the desert—for a life of solitude, prayer, fasting, and facing down the temptations of one's demons—became the ultimate display of devotion. Instead of the martyrdom of blood, choosing a hermit's life in the desert meant becoming a living witness to a life fully surrendered to God.

Although the first Christian dwellers in the deserts lived like hermits (just like Jesus spent his wilderness sojourn in solitude), the deserts of the Middle East became the places where the first Christian monasteries were established. Monasticism quickly spread throughout the Christian world, all the way to the Celtic lands in the northwest of Europe. Christianity took root in the Celtic lands through the cadences of monastic chanting and the simplicity of a communal way of life—a life imported from the desolate lands of Egypt and Palestine.

One way, then, to unpack the spiritual wisdom of the Celtic saints is to explore the mystical teachings of the desert fathers and mothers, the holy men and women who retreated into the wilderness in imitation of Jesus—only not just for forty days or so, but for their entire lives.

Is the fact that there are places called *díseart* sprinkled throughout the Celtic lands enough to establish a link between the hermits of the Middle East and the saints of Ireland, Scotland, and Wales?

The Celts left us another important clue to the esteem with which they held the spirituality of the desert. Of the high crosses found at monastic sites throughout Ireland and Scotland, many are beautifully carved, with scenes depicting events from the Old Testament, the New Testament, and the lives of Christian saints.

These crosses, which were probably colorfully painted back in the day, served the same kind of function that stained glass served in churches of a later age: as a kind of "picture book" illustrating the key events, and therefore the key beliefs, of the Christian faith.

Scholars have determined that the scene most commonly portrayed on such crosses is, of course, the crucifixion, followed by various other events from the life of Christ. But the most commonly portrayed scene on Celtic high crosses that *isn't* in the Bible depicts a legendary meeting between two renowned desert hermits: Antony of Egypt and Paul of Thebes.

Those names may not be familiar to you, but in the world of Christian monasticism, Antony and Paul are heroes of the faith. They were two of the earliest, and most respected, of the early desert dwellers, both of whom were memorialized in biographies written by their admirers. Indeed, in the *Life of Paul of Thebes*, written by Saint Jerome (famous for translating the Bible into Latin), the story of the meeting between these two famed hermits is recounted.

It's a charming story, very likely more legend than fact. But it depicts two Christians who have given everything to God, who trust mightily in the Lord for their very sustenance, and who meet one another in a spirit of humility and fraternal charity.

Why would this be the event that would capture the Celtic imagination? Why not the martyrdom of Alban (the first Christian killed for the faith in the British Isles) or the coming of Patrick to Ireland? I think it's safe to assume that the Celtic saints revered the desert fathers and mothers precisely because of how high a regard with which they held the spirituality of the desert.

So how does Celtic wisdom embody the spirituality of the desert?

Like the hermits of the Middle East, the Celtic saints valued a solitary life of seclusion and contemplation. Some, like Saint Kevin, sought to withdraw from the company of others, yearning to find God in the silence of a hermit's life. Others—again following the pattern of the desert Christians—balanced the thirst for solitude with the challenges and joys of communal living.

Like the desert elders, the earliest Celtic Christians embraced a life of austere simplicity, marked by regular prayer, fasting, and meditation. The saints of Egypt and Ireland equally understood that withdrawing into the solitude of the wilderness meant, sooner or later, wrestling with the chaos and brokenness of one's own thoughts and temptations. And finally, like the monks of the desert, Celtic Christians understood that the path to holiness was marked by repentance, humility, obedience, and immersion in the scriptures.

It's easy to romanticize "Celtic Christianity" as a kind of ancient nature mysticism, thanks to the beautiful landscape of so much of northwest Europe as well as the lyrical celebration of God's creation found in ancient Irish poetry. But it's important to remember that Celtic wisdom means more than just living in harmony with the natural world (even though that certainly forms an important part of it). For the Celtic saints, caring for the good earth was a natural outgrowth of deep devotion to God: if you are going to care for a great work of art, it begins with love for the creator.

Chapter Seven

The Cloister

In our day, Celtic spirituality has a reputation for being a spirituality grounded in the love of nature, a mystical sense of the closeness of God and/or the spiritual world, a spirituality deeply imbued with poetry and legend and storytelling, and even the "three streams" idea that Celtic wisdom provides a holistic worldview that embodies the best of both paganism and Christianity.

But for all of this—even the so-called pagan elements of Celtic spirituality—we need to acknowledge just how important monasteries and monasticism were to the ancient Celts. Not only did the earliest Celtic monks bequeath to us great art and poetry that encompasses the devotion to nature and deep mystical consciousness that we associate with Celtic Christianity, but they also recorded the pagan myths and legends associated with the Celtic peoples. Without the monks, our knowledge of Celtic wisdom, both pagan and Christian, would be impoverished if not nonexistent.

Let's take some time to consider just how important the monastic contribution is to the wisdom and spirituality of the Celtic peoples.

Along with being one of the most loved saints of the Celtic world, Brigid of Kildare was also the abbess (leader) of a great monastery. Likewise, many of the other early saints were either monks or abbots, including Saints Kevin, Brendan, Ciaran, Columcille, and Columbanus. The great Thin Places, often as not, also had monastic associations. Many of the most renowned Celtic holy sites—Kildare, Glendalough, Clonmacnoise, Skellig Michael, Iona, Lindisfarne—were the locations of early monasteries, founded during the golden age of the Celtic saints.

In the preceding chapter we looked at how important it is to understand the desert fathers and mothers in order to appreciate the unique spirituality of the Celtic saints. Now let's take that a step further. To fully appreciate Celtic wisdom, we need to explore the spirituality of the earliest Celtic monasteries. Fortunately, we have historical records, art, legends, and even architectural evidence to help us on this quest.

Our exploration begins by looking at how Celtic monasteries were similar to, and yet different from, monasteries in other parts of the Christian world. Most Christian monasteries, especially in the Western part of the church, have followed the Rule of Saint Benedict, composed in the early sixth century, as their manual for monastic living and spiritual direction. But the Benedictine Rule did not become the universal standard among Western Christians until the time of Charlemagne, in the ninth century. It is likely that the earliest Celtic Christians knew nothing of Benedict, who wasn't even born until after Saint Patrick's death. Instead, they, like other early monasteries throughout the Christian world, would have used a variety of different monastic "rules," perhaps even each monastery developing its own set of guidelines.

Indeed, a book called *The Celtic Monk* (1996) translates into English no less than nine different monastic rules originally used in ancient Irish monasteries. So like every other aspect of Celtic wisdom, Celtic monasticism was marked by diversity and the acceptance of local customs. Nevertheless, there are striking features found in most or all of the Irish rules: the Celtic monks valued austerity and self-denial; prayed continually; embraced solitude (many lived as hermits or semi-hermits); and sought to cultivate virtuous lives of humility, patience, compassion, and discipline.

It's important not to over-romanticize the ancient Celts. Some of the values and customs that the earliest monks embraced would be objectionable to most people (even monks) living today. For example, the men in particular often tried to avoid any contact with women, presumably to avoid temptation to engage in sexual fantasies or illicit sexual behavior (as if that were somehow the women's fault). Furthermore, the Celtic monks emphasized penance (acts expressing sorrow for sin), almost to the point of obsession. They stressed the importance of turning away from sinful thoughts or acts and thereby often imposed harsh conditions on themselves to express remorse for sins already committed or to reduce the risk of future sinning.

In our day, conditioned as we are by the findings of modern psychology and a Christian theology that stresses God's love and mercy rather than divine wrath, such excessive behaviors can appear to be punitive and masochistic rather than liberating. Excessively penitential behavior (which is not unique to the Celts—it is evident among the desert fathers and mothers as well) strikes the twenty-first-century reader as counterproductive and perhaps indicative of unhelpful beliefs—such as a belief that the body is somehow inferior to the spirit and must be sternly disciplined in order for a person to become holy. That seems to be dualistic or even an expression of self-contempt (hardly a spiritual value). Nevertheless, let's resist the temptation to project modern knowledge or values back on writings from 1,500 years ago. What matters is not how strict the ancient Celts were in punishing themselves for their sins— the Celts were a product of their time and culture, just like everyone else. I mention this just to highlight the fact that they were human and therefore imperfect. But what matters most is their deep faith in God and fervent desire to respond to God's love in a worthy manner.

Benedictine monasteries, especially as they evolved in the Middle Ages and beyond, often look almost like fortresses—large, imposing buildings with strict boundaries separating the monks from the people "in the world." But ancient Celtic monasteries have an entirely different design. For one thing, the earliest Celtic monasteries consisted of entire monastic "villages"—settlements where celibate men, celibate women, and families lived within the same community, arrayed around a central place of worship that formed the heart of the monastery. The monks and nuns lived separately from the families and each other, but sometimes were even under the authority of the same abbot or abbess. Saint Brigid, in particular, is renowned for being the abbess of a monastery that included both men and women. Given the patriarchal nature of the age she lived in, it is truly remarkable that she held spiritual authority over men, and perhaps represents a vestigial remnant of pre-Christian Celtic culture, where women probably enjoyed greater respect as spiritual leaders in their communities.

One of the great legacies of Celtic monasticism is the heritage of creative art—from illuminated manuscripts like *The Book of Kells* with intricate calligraphy surrounded by finely detailed designs of knotwork and spirals, to the carved high crosses covered with images taken from events in the Bible and the lives of the saints, to other precious artifacts, including ceremonial crosses, chalices, and patens used for Holy Communion. It seems that the ancient monks and nuns had a healthy appreciation for using creative talent to glorify God and to fill their lives with beauty and creativity.

Granted, this devotion to beauty is hardly unique to the Celtic world. Think of the soaring splendor of Gothic cathedrals, sprinkled across medieval Europe. But for those of us who live in the twenty-first century—a world where architecture has become utilitarian, printed books have given way to the antiseptic flash of digital e-books, and religious music has surrendered the soaring harmonies of Gregorian chants or choral polyphony in favor of bland

"Christian rock"—it's easy to forget that once upon a time, countless people gave their creative efforts to God in an act of worship and adoration. The colorful and intricately beautiful legacy of Celtic art reminds us that this is certainly true of Celtic Christians, and witnesses to an understanding of spirituality that is deeply friendly toward material things and earthly beauty.

In addition to the spirituality of the monasteries being deeply creative, it was also profoundly mystical. One interesting practice found among the Celtic Christians was an observance of what is called "the three Lents." Lent—the period of time between Ash Wednesday and Easter Sunday—is traditionally a time of spiritual preparation for Christians, with an emphasis on prayer, fasting and self-denial, and almsgiving (helping out those who are in need). It is a symbolic way for Christians to participate in the passion and death of Jesus Christ, in anticipation of the sense of celebration and joy that is marked by Christ's resurrection on Easter Sunday.

Nowadays many Christians don't bother to observe Lent at all, and even among those who do, for some it is just a time for a token sacrifice, giving up chocolate or beer or social media for the forty-day period. But ancient Christians hardly settled for such mitigated observance. They took Lent seriously and insisted that prayer, fasting, and almsgiving would be central to their religious observance during that season. And the Celts took it even a step further. The custom of the "Three Lents" involved observing three different periods of fasting, prayer, and almsgiving. In addition to the forty days prior to Easter, the forty days before Christmas and the forty days before the Feast of the Transfiguration (August 6) were also embraced as times for fasting and self-denial. What this means is that over the course of the year, about one-third of the time would be devoted to such intentional prayerful simplicity.

I don't know how widespread the observance of the Three Lents was, but it's a fascinating idea and one with an interesting parallel in the Rule of Saint Benedict. Saint Benedict wrote that a monk should live his (or her) life as if it were a perpetual Lent. In other words, to the Benedictine monk, the virtues of prayer, fasting, and almsgiving are not just special disciplines for certain seasons but should be cultivated as ongoing characteristics of a truly spiritual life.

If Benedict's idea seems a bit rigorous—especially for those of us who aren't monks or nuns—then the Celtic practice of the Three Lents might be a more attainable spiritual practice. We can all use more prayer in our lives, and perhaps we all have areas in our lives that would benefit from some appropriate extra discipline. Heaven knows we are all almost daily confronted with people in need. What if we decided to devote three forty-day seasons each year to cultivating these virtues? Wouldn't our lives—and our spirituality—more fully mature as a result? After all, spirituality is like playing a musical instrument or maintaining physical fitness; it requires regular discipline to keep us in peak form.

Spirituality is not something we do to earn God's love; it is always a response to that love, freely given. But if we are going to respond to God's freely given love, doesn't it make sense to respond as well as we are able? Observing the three Lents can be a way to do that.

Monastic spirituality has always existed at the margins of Christian life. Even in the Middle Ages when monasteries were at the height of their prestige and social influence, monks and nuns represented only a small portion of the population. After the Reformation, monasteries all but disappeared in Protestant lands and have become increasingly less prominent even in the Catholic world. I don't think the point behind Celtic spirituality is for all of us to become monks. But even non-monastics can learn something from the rhythm of prayer, honest labor, community, and simple living that characterizes the best aspects of the monastic way of life. If we want to restore the Celtic love of nature in our spiritual lives, perhaps one way to do that is by cultivating some of those "monastic" values in our lives as well.

Chapter Eight

Patrick the Enlightener

Now that we have looked at the roots of Celtic Christianity in the desert mothers and fathers, and considered the importance of monastic spirituality to the Celtic world, let's take a closer look at some of the most important Celtic saints.

We begin with a saint who is known and loved far beyond his adopted homeland of Ireland, although nowadays he is perhaps better known for the revelry that takes place on his feast day than for his spiritual wisdom or saintly life.

March 17—St. Patrick's Day—has become, in places like America, an unofficial day for celebrating

Irish culture and heritage, sort of a Gaelic alternative to the celebration of America on July 4. But beyond the tacky green party goods and "Kiss me, I'm Irish" buttons, there's a darker side to March 17: it's a date when drunk-driving arrests and alcohol-related accidents traditionally spike, at least in cities with large St. Paddy's Day celebrations.

It's a heritage that would make the saint himself sad.

If people could tear themselves away from the crowded pubs serving green-tinted beer long enough to learn about the life of Saint Patrick, they might be profoundly moved. Granted, the life of Patrick—like so many of the key players of Celtic spirituality—is shrouded in myth and legend, so much so that it's virtually impossible to separate history from fable. Some of the most charming and memorable stories associated with the saint—such as his using the shamrock to explain the Holy Trinity to the pagan Irish, or commanding the snakes to leave Ireland—belong firmly in the category of folklore.

But mythology is not meant to be history—its purpose is spiritual. Myths are told, and retold, to convey spiritual meaning at a level independent of whether a story is "true" in a scientific or scholarly sense. This is why modern fantasy novels, ranging from *The Lord of the Rings* to *The Chronicles of Narnia* and even the Harry Potter stories, touch the lives of so many people. These stories are not only entertaining tales but also mythic tales, filled with insight and inspiration regarding the meaning of life.

So let us approach the stories of Saint Patrick the same way.

We'll begin with what little we do know about this important Celtic saint. Born probably sometime in the late fourth or early fifth century, Patrick hailed from a Christian family; his father was a deacon, and his grandfather a priest (this was before celibacy became mandatory for Catholic priests). The location of Patrick's childhood home is unknown, although he probably was British, Welsh, or perhaps even Scottish. By his own admission, he was not a particularly pious child, and he blamed his spiritual indifference for the tragedy that befell him as an adolescent.

When Patrick was sixteen, pirates from Ireland captured the youth and sold him into slavery.

His pagan master forced him to work as a shepherd, meaning that the young slave often spent many hours in isolation. It was during this time that he began to more seriously attend to his spiritual life, praying and seeking God's presence. His reward? After six years of slavery, he received a locution—a mystical voice saying "Your ship is ready," instructing him to run away and seek his freedom. Traveling many miles as a fugitive, he eventually reached the coastline, where the penniless but prayerful runaway had to talk a ship's captain into giving him passage. The ship and its crew eventually landed (whether in Great Britain or mainland Europe, no one can say), and after various adventures, Patrick, now a young man in his twenties, finally returned home.

But not for long.

One night Patrick had a dream—or was it a vision?—in which a man named Victoricus came to him, from Ireland, holding "countless" letters. Taking one, Patrick read it, seeing that the letter was titled "The Voice of the Irish." As he read the letter, it seemed as if he could hear the voices of the Irish people, begging him to return to the land where he was enslaved.

Patrick reports in his autobiography that this left him heartbroken. The dream ended with him refusing or unable to read any of the many other letters. But apparently the seed was planted, and after a few years passed by, the young man—now ordained a missionary for Christ—returned to the place of his captivity and spent the rest of his life sharing the Christian Gospel with the pagan Irish and—not surprisingly—fighting human trafficking.

Was Patrick truly the first Christian to evangelize Ireland? Possibly not. Records show another missionary named Palladius served as the first bishop of Ireland, perhaps a generation or two ahead of Patrick. But for whatever reason, Patrick has captured the imagination of the Irish people, and the world, as the man who brought Christianity to Ireland. In doing so, he set the stage for elements of Celtic spirituality to be shared with the Christian community at large.

I've already mentioned Patrick's legendary reputation for pest control (at least as far as snakes are concerned); never mind that the snakes probably were separated from Ireland during the last ice age. Using the shamrock as a teaching aid is also probably just a charming legend—pagan Celtic mythology has such a strong appreciation of the number three, or "tripleness," that Patrick probably found the Irish more than willing to accept the idea that one God included three persons. But perhaps the most fascinating legend associated with the saint is the story of his breastplate, or *lorica* (from the Latin word for corselet).

In Celtic spirituality, a *lorica* is a prayer or incantation for protection. The story goes that Patrick and some fellow evangelists were traveling through an unfriendly part of Ireland, where they were at risk of being attacked by hostile warriors. As they traveled in the region, Patrick began to intone this particular supplication to keep his company safe:

> *I bind unto myself today*
> *The strong name of the Trinity,*
> *By invocation of the same,*
> *The Three in One and One in Three.*

I bind this day to me for ever,
By power of faith, Christ's Incarnation;
His baptism in the Jordan River;
His death on cross for my salvation;
His bursting from the spicèd tomb;
His riding up the heavenly way;
His coming at the day of doom;
I bind unto myself today.
I bind unto myself the power
Of the great love of the Cherubim;
The sweet 'Well done' in judgment hour;
The service of the Seraphim,
Confessors' faith, Apostles' word,
The Patriarchs' prayers, the Prophets' scrolls,
All good deeds done unto the Lord,
And purity of virgin souls.
I bind unto myself today
The virtues of the starlit heaven,
The glorious sun's life-giving ray,
The whiteness of the moon at even,
The flashing of the lightning free,
The whirling wind's tempestuous shocks,
The stable earth, the deep salt sea,
Around the old eternal rocks.

I bind unto myself today
The power of God to hold and lead,
His eye to watch, His might to stay,
His ear to hearken to my need.
The wisdom of my God to teach,
His hand to guide, his shield to ward,
The word of God to give me speech,
His heavenly host to be my guard.
. . .
Christ be with me, Christ within me,
Christ behind me, Christ before me,
Christ beside me, Christ to win me,
Christ to comfort and restore me,
Christ beneath me, Christ above me,
Christ in quiet, Christ in danger,
Christ in hearts of all that love me,
Christ in mouth of friend and stranger.
I bind unto myself the name,
The strong name of the Trinity;
By invocation of the same.
The Three in One, and One in Three,
Of whom all nature hath creation,
Eternal Father, Spirit, Word:

Praise to the Lord of my salvation,
salvation is of Christ the Lord.

(Translated by C. F. Alexander, 1889)

The legend goes that as Patrick and his company chanted this prayer for protection, they shapeshifted into a herd of deer, able to move through the woods and avoid any danger from their pagan enemies (apparently the druids were vegetarian—or, at least, not deer hunters). So now this particular poem is known as "St. Patrick's Breastplate" or "The Deer's Cry," and hymns using these words get sung in churches to this day, especially on Trinity Sunday.

It's just a fable, of course, and the *lorica* has roots in pre-Christian times as a rune or charm of protection. The historical Saint Patrick did not write these words; most scholars date "The Deer's Cry" to about the eighth century, several hundred years after Patrick's death. But it will forever be associated with the Irish saint.

So what is the wisdom of Saint Patrick? What does he have to say to us today?

Historically speaking, what really stands out is his courage—his dignity during years of enslavement, followed by taking advantage of a chance to liberate himself, only to eventually return to the very people who oppressed him, in the interest of bringing spiritual wisdom to them. The message of Christianity is one of forgiveness and mercy, and Patrick seems to embody those values well.

As for the legendary side of Patrick, the *lorica* shimmers with lyrical beauty, invoking a God who loves nature, who comes close to protect those who love Him, and who is found in all things—not only in the "stable earth, the deep salt sea, the old eternal rocks" but also in the "hearts of all that love me," and the "mouth of friend and stranger."

There are other verses of "The Deer's Cry" that are a bit harder to take, filled with fearful imagery of sin and magic that threaten to undo the one seeking God's protection. Once again, this reminds us that the Celtic saints were not perfect and that sometimes they embodied the limitations of their age. It makes sense to learn from their wisdom but also to have discernment and recognize that not every aspect of ancient Celtic spirituality needs to be promoted in our time.

For us today, Patrick—both the man and the myth—stands for a variety of spiritual values, from listening carefully to the voice of God, forgiving and helping those who have harmed us, to seeking Divine care and comfort literally in all things. It's a spirituality that calls us to deep trust and profound hope.

Chapter Nine

Brigid, Mary of the Gaels

Patrick may be the best known of the Celtic saints, but for many people, the heart of the Celtic tradition belongs to Brigid.

Legend holds that Brigid, born in the middle of the fifth century, was the daughter of a pagan chief and his Christian slave. The story goes that Brigid's mother worked in the dairy of her master's household and that she gave birth at dawn on the morning of February 1, precisely at the moment she was stepping through the door leading into the dairy.

So Brigid is very much a child of the thresholds: she was born neither in the day or the night, neither the winter nor the spring (February 1 corresponds to an ancient pagan holiday that marked the change of the seasons), neither indoors nor outdoors, neither slave nor free, neither pagan nor Christian. But you could turn this around and say that Brigid *encompasses* all of the above. She is a figure of inclusivity and hospitality.

The beginning of February corresponds to the pagan holiday of Imbolc, one of the four great agricultural festivals of the pre-Christian Celts. Perhaps it is no surprise that the mythological goddess whose cult was most associated with Imbolc was Brigit,* the daughter of the great father-god, An Dagda. An Dagda was a "Santa Claus" figure, an archetype of abundance and generosity, a big fat man with a jolly disposition who represented the desire of the ancient Celts for prosperity and plenty. So it's not surprising that Brigit (the goddess) also had a reputation as a prosperity deity, and those qualities spilled over onto Brigid (the saint).

---

* To help distinguish the goddess from the saint, I spell the goddess's name "Brigit" and the saint's name "Brigid."

Some historians even question if there ever *was* a Saint Brigid. Sir James Frazer, author of *The Golden Bough*, famously wrote, "It is obvious that St. Bride, or St. Bridget, is an old heathen goddess of fertility, disguised in a threadbare Christian cloak. Probably she is no other than Brigit, the Celtic goddess of fire and apparently of the crops." That may be a bit unfair. It makes just as much sense to see the historical Brigid as a woman, named for the pagan goddess, who embraced Christianity, or perhaps even she was a priestess of the goddess Brigit who chose to follow Christ. But this is all speculation. In the mists of what we do not know, the line separating Brigit-the-goddess and Brigid-the-saint is barely discernible. And perhaps that's the way things ought to be.

Anyway, the folklore surrounding Saint Brigid is rich and evocative. She embraced the spirituality of her mother, and even as a little girl she developed a reputation for generosity and hospitality, particularly to the poor. She worked in the kitchen, where apparently she would give food or milk or whatever she could spare to any beggar who happened to stop by. We can assume that word got out among those who relied on the kindness of strangers, and her opportunities for giving would have become more, rather than less, frequent. Eventually her father forbade her from giving any more food away. One day he put her in charge of frying some strips of bacon, and an emaciated hound appeared at the back door to the kitchen. Overcome with compassion for the stray, Brigid immediately gave the dog three of the five strips of bacon she was cooking (and which her father had counted just a few minutes earlier). Realizing her disobedience, she then prayed over the remaining bacon, and when her father stepped into the kitchen to check on her a few minutes later, he was stunned to find seven slices of bacon in the pan, rather than the original five!

The festival of Imbolc honored the lactation of farm animals, so it's not surprising that Brigid is in many ways associated with milk—beginning with her mother's work in the dairy and her own birth on the dairy threshold. As a child, she would be put in charge of churning the butter, and she would divide the butter into thirteen parts, representing Christ and the twelve apostles. The "Christ" portion she would give to the poor, saying, "I feed the poor in the name of Christ, for Christ is in the body of every poor person." She would pray over the churning as she worked, and legend has it that she could fill all the vessels of the region with the butter she churned. Even as an adult, Brigid was associated with an otherworldly cow—milky white but with red ears—that gave an endless supply of milk.

Despite these miracles of abundance associated with her, her father soon grew tired of the girl giving so much away, and so he resolved to marry her off (or sell her off as a slave, depending on which version of the story you hear). He took her to the high king and left her sitting in his wagon along with his arms (a chieftain would not carry his weapons when presenting himself before his king). As her father consulted with the king, Brigid, waiting obediently in the wagon, soon saw a beggar walking along the road. She had nothing to give him except her father's sword, which she promptly handed over, instructing the poor man to go straight into town and sell it without delay. Eventually, her father and the king came out to see the girl, but when her father noticed his sword was missing, he asked Brigid what happened, and no sooner had she said "There was this beggar . . ." than he raised his hand to strike her in anger. The king intervened, saying, "This young lady is too holy to live under my roof. I am not worthy of her." However, what he may have been thinking was something like "I'll not have her giving away *my* possessions!"

As she grew up, Brigid discerned a call to enter religious life, but her father had different ideas. He would arrange for potential suitors to come visit the attractive young woman. Finally, she took matters into her own hands—literally. One day when a suitor arrived, before presenting herself to her caller, Brigid gouged one of her eyes out of its socket, using only her bare hands. Presenting herself to the youth, he understandably turned away in horror. Once he left, Brigid promptly healed her eye, and the defiance in her gaze made her father understand that she simply would not stand for marriage. So with his reluctant blessing, she left home to establish her monastic community in *Cill Dara*—now known as Kildare, or "the Cell of the Oak." (Perhaps the oak is another pre-Christian allusion, suggesting a tree traditionally venerated by druids.)

Numerous fascinating folktales surround the establishment of the monastery in Kildare. One of the most remarkable describes how Brigid came to possess the lands for her community. She turned to the local chieftain and asked for land. He was not a particularly generous fellow, so he rather rudely suggested she could have as much land as her mantle could cover. Undeterred, Brigid took off her cloak and threw it on the ground, and the garment magically grew and grew until it covered nearly five thousand acres! Indeed, this land became known as the *Curragh*, and to this day it remains common land where livestock is raised and racehorses are trained.

Soon it came time for the bishop to come and consecrate Brigid as the abbess of her community (like other Celtic monasteries, the community in Kildare included both men and women, making Brigid a woman with spiritual authority over men—a remarkable status for a woman of the fifth-century church). The elderly bishop, Mél, came to Cill Dara with an acolyte and performed the consecration ritual outdoors (presumably under the oak tree for which Cill Dara is named). Just as he began to pray, a gust of wind blew the pages of his missal, turning from the blessing of an abbess to the consecration of a bishop. Despite the protestations of the acolyte, the aged prelate recited the words of episcopal consecration over the young nun. When finally the acolyte pointed out to Mél his error, the phlegmatic bishop commented that it must have been the doing of the Holy Spirit.

Even into the present day, Brigid is typically depicted in icons or statuary as holding a bishop's crozier. Of course, the crozier is also the staff of an abbot (or abbess), so in itself it doesn't signify much, but it does seem to reinforce the folkloric idea that this saint was not only an abbess, but a woman of true spiritual authority, equal to any bishop.

As the abbess of Kildare, Brigid soon became renowned for her holiness and spiritual leadership. The stories told about her are both charming and illuminating. Perhaps my favorite story about Brigid involves the season of Lent, the forty-day period before Easter when Christians fast in preparation for their high holy days. Brigid and two other nuns from Kildare were traveling during the Lenten season and at nightfall came to the estate of a pagan chieftain, who offered them hospitality for the night. As the three sisters sat down to share a meal with their host, they were surprised to see that their plates were filled with pork. Without a second's thought, both of the younger nuns protested, saying that their rule of life would not permit them to eat meat during Lent. Upon hearing this, Brigid stood up, grabbed each of the younger women by their arms, and escorted them out the front door of the house. She returned to the table and said to the dumbfounded pagan lord, "My apologies, good sir. My sisters are under the mistaken impression that their fast matters more than your hospitality."

Another intriguing story involves Sister Dara, a blind nun who asked for Brigid's prayers. The saint obliged, and Sister Dara's eyesight was indeed miraculously restored. But the nun discovered, to her dismay, that the ability to see physically actually hindered her mystical ability to "see" God in her soul. Distraught, the nun asked Brigid to pray for her again—only this time, to *reverse* the healing of her eyes, thereby consigning her to the beauty of darkness—a beauty in which the supernatural light of God shone.

Don't make the mistake of thinking that all of Brigid's miracles are pious in nature. Perhaps the most surprising—and yet profoundly Celtic—story, only mentioned briefly in *The Irish Life of Brigid*, tells of a woman from Kells who "hated" her husband. After Brigid intervened with prayers and some blessed holy water, the woman "loved him passionately." Some have interpreted this to suggest that Brigid is a patron saint for those who suffer from sexual dysfunction. That interpretation may be reading a bit much into the text, but we can safely assume that Brigid's legendary ability to heal included, at least for the couple from Kells, the power to help a husband and wife to love each other, joyfully and passionately.

One delightful story tells of Brigid's compassionate understanding of justice—along with her love for nature. The king of Munster had a special pet fox that had been trained to perform tricks. One day the fox got loose from the palace and ran off into the woods, where a local hunter killed the beast. When the king found out what had happened, he angrily had the man imprisoned. Hearing of this, Brigid herself went into the woods and found a wild fox; she prayed over it and the animal became docile, allowing her to carry it to the palace. She presented the fox to the king, claiming there had been a mistake and the hunter must have killed some other fox. To everyone's amazement, the new fox even performed all the same tricks as the old one. Mollified, the king released the hunter from prison. Sadly for him, though, once Brigid and the hunter left the palace, the fox reverted to its wild nature and ran off into the woods.

Some stories also link Brigid to other well-known saints of her time. One tradition suggests that she was baptized by Patrick himself. This story is not entirely unbelievable, given that Patrick is said to have lived into the second half of the fifth century, whereas Brigid was born circa 451. But the most charming encounter between Brigid and another saint involved Brendan the Navigator. Legend holds that the two knew of each other, and one time Brendan traveled from the west of Ireland to Kildare to meet the renowned abbess. When he arrived at her home, Brigid was out in the fields tending to the sheep and was caught in a rainstorm while returning to the abbey. When she arrived, the sun came back out, and she took off her soaked cloak and hung it to dry on a sunbeam shining into her room. Surprised at this, Brendan took off his own cloak and placed it next to hers on the sunbeam only to have it fall down onto the floor. Again he tried to hang it on the sunbeam, and again it fell. When it fell for the third time, he asked Brigid why her cloak hung on the sunbeam. With a twinkle in her eyes, she said, "All things are possible with prayer."

Brigid was also known as the "foster mother of Christ." I suspect this may have something to do with the esteem by which she was held among the early Celtic Christians—no woman was more honored except Mary herself (indeed, the Celts sometimes referred to Brigid as "the Mary of the Gaels"). Since Mary was Christ's actual mother, wouldn't it make sense for the second most saintly woman in all Christendom to be the Lord's foster mother? A variation of this story was that Brigid was Christ's wet nurse, which seems to hearken back to the association between Brigid (or the goddess Brigit) and milk.

It doesn't take much of a grasp of history to recognize that Brigid was born about 475 years too late to actually be Christ's wet nurse or foster mother—let alone the unlikelihood that an Irish woman could care for a baby born in Palestine. Never mind—the legend goes on to suggest that angels actually came to Brigid and carried her over the miles from Ireland to the Holy Land—simultaneously traveling backward in time—to deliver her safely to her calling to nurture Jesus in his infancy.

The Scottish painter John Duncan (1866–1945) captured a striking image of the angels carrying Brigid across the sea in his painting *Saint Bride* (1913), now on display in the Scottish National Gallery. Colorful and dramatic, the painting shows seagulls and a seal accompanying the heavenly beings (who look like they are on loan from a pre-Raphaelite painting), while Brigid, dressed in white with flowing long red hair, rests in their arms, eyes closed and hands folded in prayer. It's a fanciful image but striking in its almost otherworldly beauty.

One of the most renowned stories surrounding Brigid—and her community of nuns in Kildare—involves the tending of a sacred fire. According to Gerald of Wales, who visited Kildare in the twelfth century (centuries after Brigid's life), the nuns kept an eternal flame burning in Brigid's honor. The flame was tended on a twenty-day cycle, with one of nineteen different nuns keeping the flame burning for a twenty-four-hour period. On the twentieth day the flame was left unattended for the saint herself to watch over it, and Gerald reported that the flame never went out even when left in Brigid's care. Then again, Gerald would have had to take the nuns' word for it, as men were not allowed in the building where the flame was kept lit.

The parallels between this and pagan practices—such as the Vestal Virgins, who kept a sacred flame lit for the goddess Vesta in Rome—are obvious, and apparently bishops occasionally would instruct the nuns to extinguish the flame; but the nuns would relight it as soon as they could. It is possible that the flame was kept lit up until the time of King Henry VIII, who suppressed the monasteries as part of his program of Protestant religious reform. However, nuns in Ireland re-lit the flame in 1993, and it continues to burn in Kildare today.

I've saved my favorite Brigid story for last. A poem/prayer, attributed to Brigid but probably written sometime around the tenth century, embodies a joyful, earthy, and playful spirituality. Many translations and versions of this prayer have been made over the years; here's my paraphrase:

I would love to give a lake of beer to God almighty,
And may the Heavenly host imbibe there eternally.
I'd love the Heavenly host to live,
*   and dance, and sing with me,*
And whatever they want, I'd give to them,
*   even casks of misery.*
Radiant cups of love I'll give to them,
*   my heart more than full,*
And pitchers of mercy as well, for every one to swill.
I would make Heaven a cheerful place,
*   where happy hearts dwell,*
I'd make every one satisfied—and may
*   Jesus love me as well.*
May all the hosts of heaven gather from
*   every land and place,*
The women I'll greet with special joy,
*   the Marys of fame and grace.*
All of God's lovers will join me there,
*   by the lake of ale;*
With each sip we drink a prayer to God,
*   for ever life so hale.*

Some folktales associated with Brigid suggest that she could miraculously turn water into beer. Apparently turning water into wine was a miracle reserved for Christ alone, but Brigid could do the next best thing.

So what are we to make of Brigid today? What can we say about her, apart from the legends, folktales, and vestigial pagan myths? One way to answer that question might be to consider the ministry of the Brigidine Sisters, a Catholic women's order founded in Ireland in 1807. This is the community of sisters who still live in Kildare, where they maintain the sacred flame, operate a retreat center, and sponsor a festival dedicated to Brigid each year at the time of her feast day on February 1. The festival focuses on issues related to peacemaking and justice. I can't help but think that Brigid approves of her sacred flame still burning with an eye to hospitality, reconciliation, and community. Perhaps when we work to foster greater justice and mercy in our own communities—wherever we may live—the spirit of Celtic wisdom is embodied in our lives and our actions.

Chapter Ten

Brendan the Navigator

Different saints in the Celtic tradition embody different qualities of Celtic spirituality and wisdom. Patrick represents the gift of a profound faith, which enabled him to survive years of slavery, to return to the land where he was enslaved, and to give his life to sharing his wisdom and fighting the very injustices that he had suffered under. By contrast, Brigid represents the richness of Celtic hospitality, generosity, and kindness.

Now let's turn to one of the most storied of Celtic saints, one who was renowned throughout Europe during the Middle Ages for his almost magical story of adventure at sea. Saint Brendan of Clonfert, who lived from circa 484 to about 577, earned himself the nickname "Brendan the Navigator" because of his wondrous sea voyage. He is the patron saint of sailors, mariners, divers, and other boatmen. He embodies both the spirit of Celtic wanderlust and a deep mystical thirst for God, a thirst to find (and inhabit) heaven on earth.

Hailing from County Kerry in the southwest of Ireland, young Brendan received his earliest Christian faith formation from a nun, Ita of Killeedy. After five years with Saint Ita, Brendan—still a boy—was sent to a monastery school, and after finishing his education was ordained a priest and established a series of monasteries in the Celtic lands, traveling throughout the west coast of Ireland and journeying to Scotland, Wales, and even Brittany in mainland Europe. But his most famous voyage took him not east to Europe, but west over the open sea. That story is chronicled in an ancient text known as *Navigatio Sancti Brendani Abbatis*—or *The Voyage of Saint Brendan the Abbot*.

The *Navigatio* is about as close as you can get to a medieval bestseller. Over one hundred ancient manuscript copies of the text have been preserved, showing that it was widely copied, and we may assume widely read, in medieval times. The story of Brendan's journey conforms to a genre of Celtic literature and mythology called the *Immrama*, or the "wondrous sea voyages." Many such tales extend all the way back into pagan mythology, where godlike figures with exotic names such as Bran the Blessed or Mael Duin set sail from the west coast of Ireland, heading out over the boundless sea in search of an earthly paradise. Indeed, some scholars speculate that the ancient Irish seafarers may have made it all the way to Greenland or even Newfoundland, which would make *them*, not Leif Erikson or Christopher Columbus, the first Europeans to reach North America.

This story raises the question of whether the *Navigatio* is factual or mythological. For now, let's set that question aside, because regardless of how *historical* this story may (or may not) be, the *spiritual wisdom* found in it remains meaningful.

Unlike its pagan counterparts, *The Voyage of Brendan the Abbot* is a thoroughly Christian tale; its protagonist is not a pagan god, but the abbot of a

Christian monastery. Likewise, the adventures have a clearly Christian and even monastic theme, with the goal of the voyage—the so-called land of promise—representing a mythical place where heaven is on earth.

The story begins one day when a friend of Brendan's comes to visit him in his cloister and announces that he has just returned from his own voyage where he sailed west, all the way to the land of promise—in other words, to paradise on earth itself.

Brendan, not surprisingly, finds this news entrancing, and after considering the matter in his own prayers, resolves to sail himself, with several of his monks as companions, in their own quest for this earthly paradise. And thus begins a charming, if fantastic, tale of visiting a variety of islands over the course of seven years at sea, many of which are inhabited by monks (naturally), while others represent a variety of unusual or even magical settings: one features a choir of birds who chant the psalms, while another is an uninhabited island where nevertheless a mystical hospitality occurs, with a dining hall featuring food mysteriously prepared and served for all the voyagers. Along the way, Brendan and his company have narrow escapes from whales and sea serpents, and in one dramatic episode of their story, they find the very mouth of hell itself, replete with fire, brimstone, and swirling demons. At another time they encounter none other than Judas Iscariot, whom they find chained to a rock in a stormy sea, where he is lashed by waves every Sunday. As awful as that sounds, for Judas this is actually a respite from his normal, far worse torments in hell. The condemned biblical figure tells Brendan that the demons chain him to the rock every Sunday, so it represents his sabbath rest, which he receives each week after enduring the fires of hell for the preceding six days.

Finally, Brendan and his company reach the very island of paradise itself, filled with glittering jewels, abundant fruit, and an angel who turns them back noting that they must return to Ireland to live out the rest of their mortal lives, before finally returning to the promised island for all eternity.

So after a short visit to the land of promise, Brendan and his companions return home, where he commits his tale to writing and spends the rest of his days in prayer and contemplation.

If you are a fan of C. S. Lewis's Narnia stories, the voyage of Brendan might strike you as familiar—and with good reason. One of the tales of Narnia concerns the adventures of the *Dawn Treader*, a ship that sails over the Narnian ocean, under the direction of King Caspian, undergoing many adventures along the way, but leading ultimately to the very end of the Narnian world, beyond which lies Aslan's country—the Narnian paradise.

Despite some significant differences between *The Voyage of Brendan the Abbot* and C. S. Lewis's *The Voyage of the Dawn Treader*, the similarities in both plot and detail are so numerous that we could argue that C. S. Lewis has actually made his own twentieth-century contribution to the literature of the *Immrama*. Lewis himself admitted, in his notes, that the story of the *Dawn Treader* was inspired by Ulysses and Saint Brendan. The relationship between the adventures of Saint Brendan and the *Dawn Treader* becomes clearer when we consider that the *Navigatio* represents far more than merely some sort of amusing medieval adventure. In fact, the story consists of an allegorical tale of monastic formation and growth in the Christian spiritual life. Monastic values such as obedience, humility, hospitality, the recitation of daily prayer, the chanting of psalms, and the observance of the liturgical year all form the skeleton of Brendan's adventure. It's a grand metaphor for earthly life as a spiritual pilgrimage, all of which may be seen as a voyage from birth to death—the point of departure into the mystery of eternity. By joining Brendan in the "ship" of his monastery, monks who seek the paradise of heavenly promise are offered passage, in the context of prayer and monastic life. Likewise, those who read the story of Saint Brendan and try to apply its moral to their life—recognizing that prayer, perseverance, and faithfulness are the compass points to help us navigate the stormy waters of earthly life—may find their own safe passage to the island of promise, waiting for them just on the other side of death.

Incidentally, C. S. Lewis is generally considered to be an English writer, since he spent most of his life living in Britain and teaching at Oxford or Cambridge. But he was born in Belfast and was in fact half Irish. So it is fair to see him as a twentieth-century figure standing in the great tradition of Celtic spirituality, and *The Voyage of the Dawn Treader* makes that explicit.

Unlike Brendan, Lewis was no monk and had no reason to write a morality tale based on the virtues of the cloistered life. But he did consider *The Voyage of the Dawn Treader* to be an illustration of the life-long project of Christian spirituality. In a letter he wrote to a schoolgirl named Anne Jenkins in 1961, Lewis remarks that *The Voyage of the Dawn Treader* depicts "the spiritual life (specially in Reepicheep)."

King Caspian may have been the leader of the *Dawn Treader's* expedition, but his faithful servant—Reepicheep, the valiant talking mouse—actually is the most "Brendan-like" figure on the voyage; for it is Reepicheep who explicitly joins the expedition because he is seeking Aslan's country and (spoiler alert) at the end of the tale is the only member of the crew to sail all the way there, never to return to Narnia.

The British author Evelyn Underhill wrote that the Christian mystical life consists of five stages: awakening, purification, illumination, the dark night of the soul, and union with God. This map, or itinerary, of the spiritual life did not originate with Underhill; rather, she builds her developmental description of the mystical life on a classic threefold formulation of spiritual growth, consisting of purgation, followed by illumination, leading to union. This threefold way can be traced back at least as far as the third century, as it is developed by Origen of Alexandria, who died circa 254.

This map corresponds precisely to the plot of *The Voyage of the Dawn Treader*, although not all of the action concerns Reepicheep the mouse. Eustace, the ill-mannered English schoolboy, provides the context of how Lewis depicts both the spirituality of awakening and purification, whereas Lucy's adventures on an island of silence illustrates the spirituality of illumination, culminating in an appearance by Aslan himself. The entire ship visits an island enshrouded in darkness, Lewis's way of depicting the dark night of the soul. After the Eucharistic symbolism on the Island of the Three Sleepers, some of the most beautiful prose in the Narnia books—or arguably, throughout Lewis's entire corpus—describes the *Dawn Treader's* voyage into a silver sea filled with silence and light, culminating, for Reephicheep alone, in the final voyage to Aslan's country itself, representing the ultimate beatitude of union with God.

I've spent all this time veering away from Saint Brendan to talk about Narnia simply because Brendan's adventure, steeped as it is in medieval and monastic symbolism, may not be as immediately accessible to twenty-first-century readers as is Lewis's charming tale of the *Dawn Treader*. But if Lewis did an excellent job at explaining the dynamics of a lifelong spiritual journey using the metaphor of a sea voyage, he had Saint Brendan (and the earlier, pagan *Immrama*) to thank. Lewis's tale is a salient illustration of how Celtic wisdom has remained relevant and meaningful over the centuries, even if it requires new stories to be told and new ways of thinking about its core values.

So how does the story of Saint Brendan make a difference for you and me? Consider how your life is a journey. It's not over yet—which means you are still "at sea," still navigating both the blessings and the challenges of your journey. Like Brendan, you are called to keep your eyes on the prize (whether that is heaven on earth, or simply a life filled with wisdom, love, and joy) and to make prayer, perseverance, and faith your touchstones as you continue to navigate toward your goal.

Chapter Eleven

Columcille, Saint in Exile

Ireland is said to have three patron saints. Patrick is one, of course, as the legendary first apostle to the Irish; and another is Brigid, clearly the most-loved and storied of women Celtic saints. The third patron is Columba—or Columcille, to use the Irish version of his name—who might seem a bit odd as a patron of Ireland, since he is best known as a missionary to Scotland.

Columcille means "the dove of the church," a name with echoes of the Holy Spirit and of peace-making. Born in late 521 in County Donegal in the north of Ireland, Columcille came from the prominent Uí Néill family, related to Irish royalty. He received his formation as a monk under the tutelage of Saint Finnian of Clonard, but also was educated by an Irish bard named Gemman. Eventually, Columcille took his monastic vows and was ordained a deacon and later a priest. He was involved in establishing several monasteries in Ireland and became known as one of the "twelve apostles of Ireland." But his earthly renown would soon lead to disaster.

Sometime around the year 560, Columcille became involved in several religious and political disputes. He visited the monastery of Finnian of Movilla and copied a psalter (a book of the Psalms) without the abbot's permission. When Finnian demanded that the copied psalter remain at Movilla, a legal conflict ensued, what is now considered one of the first copyright disputes in Western history. Finnian insisted that because he owned the original psalter, he had the right to decide if it could be copied and by whom, whereas Columcille insisted that because he had copied the book, the copy was rightly his. Eventually, the King of Ulster weighed in, deciding for Finnian. Unwilling to accept defeat,

Columcille took his grievance back to the Uí Néill family, setting into motion events that led to a political uprising—and a bloody battle between the king's warriors and the Uí Néills, resulting in many deaths.

Church leaders were outraged, and some called for Columcille's excommunication. But with others speaking on his behalf, a synod decreed that he should go into exile. Conscience-stricken by the loss of life, Columcille agreed, declaring that he intended to evangelize as many people as had died in the battle. Shortly thereafter he left Ireland for Scotland; in the last thirty-four years of his life, he returned to his homeland only once.

Columcille and his companions established a new monastery on a small island in the Hebrides, an archipelago off the west coast of Scotland. This island, Iona, became renowned as a great center of prayer and learning, and to this day is honored as a place where Celtic wisdom and spirituality continue to thrive. One of the greatest treasures of Celtic art, *The Book of Kells*, was created or at least begun in Iona (it eventually was sent to Kells, in the mainland of Ireland, to protect it from Viking marauders). Great kings were buried on Iona, including the historical Macbeth (whose real life wasn't nearly as dramatic as it was fictionalized by Shakespeare). Columcille's monastery survived for centuries, and helped to bring Christianity to mainland Scotland and northern England. In the twentieth century, a Scottish clergyman named George Macleod established the Iona Community, an ecumenical group that restored Iona Abbey, making it a world-famous retreat center and pilgrimage site.

As with saints Patrick and Brigid, there is much folklore surrounding Columcille, and while much of it may be legendary, it is all insightful into the heart of Celtic wisdom. Columcille is said to have had particular affinity with animals. According to one story, the abbot gathered the brothers of the monastery together and told them that, in three days time, a crane from Ireland would land on the beach of Iona. He instructed the monks to care for the exhausted bird; after feeding it for three days, it would be ready to fly home—which it did. According to this legend, Columcille could foretell the arrival of the bird because it came from Ireland, so great was his love for his homeland.

Another story tells of a horse that wept when Columcille was near death. When the elderly saint sat down to rest while out for a walk, a workhorse that belonged to the monastery's dairy came up to him and laid its head on the saint's chest, where it proceeded to shed tears of sorrow. Columcille's biographer, Adomnán, said that the horse even uttered cries of sadness at the impending death of its master. A monk who saw the horse's behavior tried to shoo it away from the frail abbot, but Columcille intervened. "Let it be, since it is fond of me; allow it to express its grief." The saint blessed the sad horse and died shortly thereafter.

But perhaps the most remarkable animal tale associated with Saint Columcille concerns what may very well be the earliest sighting of the Loch Ness monster. Also reported by Adomnán, the story goes that the saint was staying with the Picts—a group of Celts who inhabited ancient Scotland—and came upon some of the locals burying a body near the River Ness. Apparently, the dead man had been attacked and drowned by a ferocious "water beast." One of Columcille's brother monks went down into the water to investigate, and the beast appeared, but when Columcille made the sign of the cross and commanded the monster to leave, it disappeared.

While it's easy to dismiss this as yet another bit of medieval folklore, those who believe in the existence of the Loch Ness monster will cite this story as evidence that the creature has lived in those waters for many centuries (even though it is usually associated with the lake [loch] rather than the River Ness).

Columcille loved not only animals but also trees and woodlands. In fact, he once remarked that he feared the sound of an axe in the woods of Derry more than he feared hell itself.

Columcille is also famous for describing Christ as his "arch-druid." This may have been part of his effort to spread Christianity among the pagans of Scotland, by suggesting that Christ was a better druid than the druids. But it's a tantalizing glimpse into how the three streams—particularly the pagan and the Christian streams of Celtic spirituality— seem to join together. Rather than suggesting that Christ and Christianity are simply opposed to the ancient wisdom of the Celts, to call Christ an arch-druid suggests that a deep harmony between the indigenous, nature-centered spirituality of the pre-Christian Celts and the imported mysticism of the Jewish rabbi revered as the son of God may truly be at the heart of the wisdom the Celts offer the world today.

It is said that Columcille never went an hour without engaging in spiritual pursuits such as study or prayer. Certainly, as a monk, he gave his entire life to the web of chanting and prayer that characterizes the deep spirituality of the cloister. But for us today, Columcille also represents the possibility of forging a new life, even after a terrible disaster. It must not have been easy for him to go from being one of the most prominent figures in the Irish Church, the scion of a royal family, to the austere life of a humble abbot on a tiny windswept island off the coast of Scotland, exiled from his homeland, ashamed that his actions led to the spilling of blood. Yet it was the final three decades of his life, as the apostle to Scotland, that ultimately formed his character—no longer the proud and fiery youth, but a mellower, humbler, deeply prayerful man in his maturity. Columcille stands in the line of many Christians—from Matthew the tax collector to Paul the persecutor to Augustine the libertine, and beyond—who reinvented their lives, by the grace of God, even after making a terrible mistake. If they could do it, so could you and I, even if our mistakes are not always as great as theirs. But many people struggle with feelings of remorse, regret, or shame after having done things that have caused suffering or harm to others (or to ourselves). Columcille is the saint for all who sorrow for their past mistakes. He stands for the willingness to "go into exile" (in other words, make a radical new start) and accept the grace to create a new and better life, marked by humility and filled with gratitude.

Chapter Twelve

For All the Saints

Ireland has been called "the island of saints and scholars." But the other Celtic lands all have produced their share of holy people as well. The coming of Christianity to the Celtic world was revolutionary on more than one level. Not only did Christianity deepen and expand the way that the Celts expressed their spirituality and their understanding of life, but perhaps just as importantly, the Celtic tradition influenced how Christianity was practiced, at least among the Celts—giving birth to a unique expression of that faith, marked by optimism, mysticism, and deep love for nature.

Saint Patrick is arguably the most well known of the Celtic saints, which is to say he is a saint whose fame and popularity extends well beyond the Celtic world. But the other saints we have considered—Brigid, Columcille, and Brendan the Navigator—all have enjoyed their own measure of fame. But these four have not even begun to exhaust the treasury of Celtic holy men and women whose poetry, lives, and renowned holiness can continue to inspire us today.

What's truly lovely about the Celtic world is the abundance of lesser-known saints, many of whom are remembered and venerated in only one particular region. Many of the oldest saints were never officially canonized by the Church, but that has not stopped their small-scale cults from flourishing. In a way, the Celtic devotion to saints echoes the older pagan veneration of gods and goddesses—the emphasis was not on the big names that everyone knew, but on the local figure who may never have been famous but who gave a particular place its own unique sanctity.

In this chapter we'll look at some of the lesser-known, but still truly remarkable, Celtic holy men and women, with an eye to the great variety by

which the Celtic peoples responded to the call of
holiness in their lives.

❧ ❧ ❧

The monk and evangelist Mungo, also known as
Kentigern, lived in the sixth century. Of noble British birth, he became a missionary in northwest
England and Scotland, and is today perhaps best
known as the founder and patron saint of Glasgow.
The city's coat of arms includes four symbols associated with Mungo: a bird, a fish, a bell, and a tree. The
bell commemorates a legend in which the saint received a bell as a gift from the pope, while the three
symbols from nature each correspond to a miracle
associated with Mungo. The bird symbolizes a robin
that Mungo raised from the dead; the tree represents
a miraculous fire he kindled with frozen wood;
while the fish depicts a salmon he caught that had
the queen's lost ring in its belly, thereby saving her
from her husband's wrath.

The nature symbols correspond to the three great
realms of nature: the fish represents the lower regions
of water (sea, river, lake, well); the bird represents

the upper regions of the atmosphere (the sky); while the tree symbolizes the land herself. Land, sea, and sky: one of many sacred Celtic trinities. Like many of the Celtic saints, Mungo reminds us that nature is a gift from God and that we can find spiritual meaning even in the humblest of things.

Mungo spent time in Wales but eventually returned to Glasgow and was buried at the site of Glasgow Cathedral, where today the crypt is still said to house his remains.

◦ ◦ ◦

We met Ita briefly when we looked at her most famous pupil: Brendan the Navigator. Now let's take a closer look at the teacher herself.

Ita was the abbess of a monastic community located in County Limerick, Ireland. She has been described as the "Brigid of Munster," suggesting that she played a role in the south of Ireland similar to that held in the east by her more famous contemporary. This marketing trick is as dangerous today as it was a thousand years ago: compare yourself to someone more famous, and you're at risk for never getting out of that person's shadow. Even so, Ita remained a popular saint in the south of Ireland and will forever be immortalized for her role as Brendan's first teacher. The Navigator continued to seek her counsel long after leaving her fosterage. Unlike the many Celtic saints who were famed for their travels, Ita apparently loved the place where she first put down roots and remained in Limerick until her death in the year 570.

It is said that one of the most important things any of us can do is raise or teach a child well. Perhaps Ita should be the patron saint of those who nurture greatness among those of the next generation.

᛫᛭ ᛫᛭ ᛫᛭

Piran is the patron saint of Cornwall and of tin miners (the tin trade being particularly important in that region); some historians speculate that he may be the same figure as the Irish saint Ciaran, the founder of the monastery at Clonmacnoise. Legend holds that Piran once escaped from captivity in Ireland and sailed to Cornwall using a millstone for a raft! Apparently, the good saint had quite the capacity to work miracles; after all, sailing a stone boat makes even walking on water seem, well, easy.

Today, scholars question just how historical a figure he is, wondering if, like other Celtic figures such as Brigid and even Patrick, his story may actually reflect more myth than fact. Maybe it does, but in the Celtic world, myth matters. Celtic spirituality envisions a world where anything is possible—where saints can cause a millstone to float or perform all sorts of other miracles. Why believe in such impossible tales? What good can possibly come out of crazy tales of miracles and floating rocks? We know that the human mind is an amazing instrument, and that often the key to extraordinary events, such as a scientific discovery, breaking an athletic record, or summoning superhuman strength at a moment of crisis, begins with the power to believe. If we allow ourselves to imagine a world of wonders, a world where a saint could make a millstone float, it opens up just a glimmer of possibility—what Joseph Chilton Pearce called "the crack in the cosmic egg"—that allows miracles to happen. Just because we believe.

⚬ ⚬ ⚬

Of all the Celtic saints, the one who seems to be the most like the renowned Saint Francis of Assisi (patron saint of animals) is probably Saint Kevin, who seems to have gotten along better with animals than with his fellow human beings. Numerous legends and stories are associated with the reclusive founder of Glendalough, underscoring his reputation as a friend of nature and a lover of animals.

One tale recounts how the saint was praying by one of the lakes near his hermitage when his prayer book slipped and fell into the water. Even today such a turn of events would be an annoyance, but consider how in ancient times books were rare, valuable, and difficult to replace; this would have been a true catastrophe. But before Kevin could even jump in after the book, an otter, sensing the sanctity and compassion of the man, grasped the book and returned it to its owner. Other stories tell of bears seeking refuge from hunters in the cave Kevin used as his hermitage, and of birds coming to perch on his shoulders or his head while the saint stood quietly at prayer. One day while praying, Kevin discovered that a blackbird had begun to build a nest on his outstretched hand. Filled with compassion, he could not bear to disturb her motherly work, and so stood still as she completed her nest, laid her eggs, and eventually hatched and raised her young. Finally, when the babies were old enough to fly, Kevin at long last allowed his arms to rest.

Will you be called to stand still at prayer for weeks while a bird nurtures her young? Probably not. But we can look to Kevin and prayerfully consider how, in more humble and down-to-earth ways, each of us can foster a more caring and sustainable relationship with the world of nature.

❧ ❧ ❧

March 1 marks the feast day of the patron saint of Wales, Dewi (or David), who died on that day in 588. Known for his austerity and simplicity, Dewi founded a monastery where no wine was drunk nor meat consumed, and work was largely done in silence. As a bishop, Dewi worked hard to preserve the autonomy of the Celtic church in Wales from the encroaching power of the more Roman-style Christians of Saxon England; he is also credited with refuting the Pelagian heresy during his ministry (Pelagius was a British theologian whose ideas were eventually denounced as heresy, particularly by Saint Augustine). According to legend,

Dewi founded twelve monasteries and eventually he traveled to Jerusalem, where he was consecrated an archbishop. But as is so often the case in the legends of the Celtic saints, these stories may not be historically factual. Despite his reputation as a strict and austere monk, Dewi's dying words may be the best insight into his character, and clearly reveal how the saint embodied the delightful charm of the Celtic spirit: "Brothers and sisters, be joyful and keep the faith." Perhaps meditation on those words may be the best way for us to integrate Dewi's wisdom in our lives today.

⊕　⊕　⊕

Aside from Iona, perhaps the most storied place associated with Celtic spirituality in Great Britain is Lindisfarne, the "Holy Isle" on the northwest coast of England. Several saints are particularly associated with Lindisfarne, including Cuthbert and Aidan. From early in his life, Cuthbert of Lindisfarne was a visionary; according to the English historian Bede, Cuthbert's gift began with a vision he received the night of Aidan of Lindisfarne's death. At the request of a Northumbrian king, Aidan had left the monastery at Iona to found the Celtic monastic community at Lindisfarne. At the time of Aidan's death in August 651, the adolescent Cuthbert was a shepherd; while watching over his flock, he saw the angels escorting Aidan to heaven. This event inspired him to enter the monastic life as well. In due course, his journey took him to Lindisfarne, where he eventually served as prior before retreating to a nearby island to live a hermit's life. But like Kevin of Glendalough, he continually was sought out by those who had heard of his holiness, and so eventually he accepted the call to be consecrated bishop of the Holy Isle. Also like Kevin, he had a reputation as a friend of animals, and his ministry was characterized by gentleness and care for the poor. He died only two years after his consecration as a bishop; today his remains are buried in Durham Cathedral, after having been relocated repeatedly to hide them from the Vikings.

It's sad that many people do not associate gentleness with Christian spirituality, but Cuthbert, who was famed for his tenderness and kindness to the monks who lived with him, reminds us that sometimes a gentle word or kind action may be the wisest course to take.

◦ ◦ ◦

Another Welsh saint, Winefride, has a particularly gruesome story associated with her. Legend holds that she was born into a noble family, and her uncle, Beuno, also is revered as a saint. As a young woman, Winifride was courted by a man named Caradoc, but she decided that she didn't want to marry and would become a nun. Caradoc responded to her rebuff by taking out his sword and beheading the young woman. Her head hit the ground and rolled away (I warned you that this was gory). But where it came to rest, a holy well sprung forth. Meanwhile, Uncle Beuno retrieved her head and prayed for her healing, and she was restored to life (although with a scar marking the place of her wound). Meanwhile, the uncle prayed for justice against Caradoc, who was struck dead on the spot—legend holds that the earth swallowed his body whole. Winefride did go on to become a nun, and later an abbess, and eventually retired from the abbey to a life of solitary prayer.

What I love about Winefride's story, legendary though it may be, is that even after the remarkable event of being martyred and then resurrected, the saint goes on to lead an ordinary and obscure life of prayer and meditation. She is an example for us all that spirituality is not about fame and fortune, but about a life lived authentically and well.

~ ~ ~

Many saints populated the Celtic church: Colman, of Iona and Lindisfarne, who retreated to a remote foundation in Ireland rather than submit to Roman authority; Enda of Inishmore, one of the earliest Irish monks who mentored Ciaran of Clonmacnoise and advised Brendan the Navigator; Yves Hélory, a Breton lawyer who became canonized because of the kindness he showed to the poor; Maughold, a pirate converted to Christianity who established a great monastery on the Isle of Man; Adomnán, who became a soul friend to Irish kings and the best-known biographer of Columcille. The list could go on and on. Every Celtic saint, famous or humble, stands for celebrating the rich tradition of spiritual devotion and reminds every one of us, ordinary mortals though we might be, to live a life of sanctity and spiritual virtue—yes, even now. Celtic spirituality is the spirituality of intimacy and closeness between the mortal and heavenly worlds. If the spiritual realm is so available to us, then also holiness is within each person's grasp. You don't have to be as famous as Patrick or Columcille to manifest the life of devotion. Simply choosing to do it is all it takes to get started on the journey. It's a long and arduous journey, mind you—but a path that has been trod by many worthy feet before us.

PART THREE

Walking the Celtic Path

DHE, beannaich an ce 's na bheil ann,
Dhe, beannaich mo cheile is mo chlann,
Dhe, beannaich an re a ta 'na m' cheann,
Is beannaich, a Dhe, laimhseachadh mo laimh;
An am domh eirigh 's a mhaduinn mhoich,
Is laighe air leabaidh anamoich,
    Beannaich m' eirigh 's a mhaduinn mhoich,
    Is mo laighe air leabaidh anamoich.
Dhe, teasruig an teach 's an t-ardrach,
Dhe, coistrig a chlann mhathrach,
Dhe, cuartaich an spreidh 's an t-alach;
Bi-sa fein na'n deigh 's da'n taladh,
Duair dhireas ni ri frith 's ri fruan,
Duair shineas mi a sios an suan,
    Duair dhireas ni ri frith 's ri fruan,
    Duair shineas mi an sith gu suan.

GOD, bless the world and all that is therein.
God, bless my spouse and my children,
God, bless the eye that is in my head,
And bless, O God, the handling of my hand;
What time I rise in the morning early,
What time I lie down late in bed,
    Bless my rising in the morning early,
    And my lying down late in bed.
God, protect the house, and the household,
God, consecrate the children of the motherhood,
God, encompass the flocks and the young;
Be Thou after them and tending them,
What time the flocks ascend hill and wold,
What time I lie down to sleep,
    What time the flocks ascend hill and wold,
    What time I lie down in peace to sleep.

—*Carmina Gadelica*

Chapter Thirteen

Hospitality

As inspiring as the stories of the great Celtic saints are, how do we make the spirituality and wisdom of the Celtic people meaningful today? In this, and the next four chapters, we'll explore five approaches to *practical* Celtic spirituality, including the gift of hospitality, the beauty of soul friendship, the power of poetry and storytelling, the energy of wisdom, and the treasures that await us if only we dare to embrace the search. Read these final chapters with an eye to making Celtic wisdom your own. This spirituality is more than just legends from the past; it represents a holistic and visionary way of seeing and being in the world that promises to infuse even the most mundane aspects of life with the joy that comes only from the heart of God—a joy that comes to us both through the wisdom of the past and the splendor of nature.

In addition to these chapters, I encourage you to revisit Chapter Five, "The Edge of Waiting." The Celtic approach to contemplation is so foundational to this wisdom tradition that I felt it needed to be presented toward the beginning of this book, but *rinn-fheitheamh* (contemplative prayer) also deserves to be included among the practices of Celtic spirituality.

◈ ◈ ◈

From pre-Christian times, the Celts recognized hospitality as a core value of their civilization. The reigns of mythic kings were judged on their hospitality (or lack thereof). Once, when Bres, a warrior of the Fomorian people—the "bad guys" of Celtic myth—became king of the Tuatha Dé Danann, he quickly became renowned for his parsimony. Bards complained that visitors to his house could count on leaving with no smell of beer on their breath! Soon, a bard named Cairbre was fed up enough to write a satire about the ungenerous king—the first satire ever composed in Ireland. Its effect was blistering—literally—as it caused sores to burst forth on Bres's face, blemishing him and making him unfit to rule.

I don't think the message here is about taking revenge on those we encounter who lack hospitality. Like charity, hospitality begins at home, and so the story of Bres is a reminder that if we want to live in a world of hospitality, we begin by opening our own doors (and hearts). Fortunately, the Celts have been (and still are) masters at hospitality.

A few years back I attended a workshop featuring the Celtic author Caitlín Matthews. At one point during the program, the question of religious tolerance came up. Matthews spoke for a minute or two about the many different kinds of people who attend her workshops, ranging from Christians to pagans. Likewise, she noted that she presented her programs in a variety of settings, from Catholic convents to Wiccan covens. She concluded, "I'm willing to speak anywhere where a spirituality of hospitality is practiced." Those words gave me a clear sense of how Celtic wisdom transcends religious boundaries. Hospitality does not erase religious (or any other) differences. But within the gracious gesture of hospitality, our tribal identities cease to become the defining factor of who we are. If I am focusing on how you and I are so different from one another, relationship and community become strained if not impossible. But when we choose to place our attention instead on our kinship and on what we share with open hearts, then our differences are reduced to the simple ways in which we embody diversity and distinctiveness—lovely qualities, after all, for they have their roots in nature.

What does it mean, then, to practice hospitality? On one level, it's as simple as welcoming those who enter into our lives, whether as guests in our homes, pilgrims passing through our communities, or newcomers to our homeland. To be hospitable means welcoming those who come to us, whether because they need our help or simply want to enjoy our company. Hospitality is linked to generosity and kindness—as the story of Bres makes clear, one cannot be hospitable if one behaves in a miserly manner.

Celtic myth suggests hospitality places demands on those who *receive* it as well as those who *give* it. In other words, to refuse another's hospitality is itself a breach of hospitality. A sacred vow or *geas* bound Cúchulainn, the great hero of Ulster, never to refuse hospitality. Many such heroes had one or more *geasa* imposed on them, prohibiting them from certain acts lest tragedy ensue if the *geas* were broken. Alas for Cúchulainn, he had another *geas*, never to eat the meat of a dog. The moment of truth came when he encountered an impoverished old woman who offered him a bowl of stew. The gruel contained hound meat. Faced with an impossible dilemma, Cúchulainn finally accepted the food and ate the meat, even though this act set into motion the events that would claim his life. Disregarding for a moment the larger themes of tragedy in that story, consider how Cúchulainn, knowing that he would break a vow no matter what he did, chose to preserve hospitality rather than maintain the purity of his diet. I'm not trying to suggest that a diabetic should eat a candy bar just because someone offers it, but simply that the Celtic heart regards hospitality with such honor that even a warrior as mighty as Cúchulainn couldn't bear to refuse it.

We've already seen how Saint Brigid and two nuns from her convent were on the road one year during Lent and were offered hospitality by a pagan chieftain. At the evening meal, the host served pork to the sisters, and the younger nuns said they couldn't eat it for fear of breaking their Lenten fast. At that, Brigid stood up, grabbed each of the sisters, and forcibly hurled them out of the house. She returned to table, apologized to the host for their behavior, and proceeded to enjoy her pork dinner. To the saint, respecting hospitality mattered more than maintaining a religious fast.

Celtic hospitality is not just a matter of folklore and legend. One time I was in Banbridge, County Down, and couldn't find lodging. I mentioned this to the owner of a pub, and he spent the next half hour driving me around until I found a room for the night. An even better tale comes from a former student of mine, who had a flat tire once while traveling in rural Ireland. Stopping in front of a farmhouse and hoping to use the phone, he met the farmer, who insisted on fixing the tire himself, and then the farmer's wife invited my student and his family in for dinner. And, of course, talk of payment was quickly squelched. "No need for that," the farmer said simply.

Maybe in some parts of the world these stories would be unremarkable. But to an American used to living in a rapid-paced urban environment where too few people really reach out to others, such stories of hospitality are as inspiring as sadly unfamiliar. May the wisdom of the Celts help all of us to reclaim a more welcoming way of life.

True hospitality can only be given freely, and it extends far beyond material generosity. A corporation will give away tremendous resources in its promotional campaigns, but this giving is always done with an eye to future sales and profits. Meanwhile, true hospitality can be found in a moment of attention or a simple glass of water on a sweltering day. Perhaps the single most important quality in hospitality is freedom. If I give in order to receive later, it's not a free gift, and I remain indentured to my own need for self-protection. Only when I am truly free am I in a position to open my life to receive the stranger and support those who come to me with a need—without conditions or strings attached. That's when hospitality happens.

Likewise, true hospitality can exist only when we also maintain appropriate boundaries, not to mention common sense. Cúchulainn may have understood the importance of hospitality, but he was also a warrior. Needless to say, he didn't roll out the welcome mat when an army invaded Ulster. There's no point in becoming imprisoned by the role of host. The minute we feel obligated to be generous, what we are doing is something different from hospitality. Maybe it's saving face, or keeping up appearances, or trying to please Mom or God or someone. Such behavior may not be bad—but it's not true hospitality. So don't check your brain at the door. You're only free to say yes when you are equally free to say no.

How can we practice hospitality today? We may not be persons who regularly have pilgrims knocking at our door seeking a night's lodging (unless we manage a B&B), but we all have situations in our lives when we are called to respond to the needs of a stranger. Someone may need assistance with a dead battery or a health emergency. Refugees may need support when they relocate to our city. A parent or grandparent may need help to make the unwanted transition into assisted living or nursing home care. These, and many other situations, intrude upon our day (or our lives). Each one invites us to embrace (or refuse) the gift of hospitality: do we meet the person who comes to us in need with grace and generosity, or do we provide subtle (or not so subtle) signals that we wish they had left us alone? No one is perfect, of course, but if you are interested in the wisdom of the Celts, take inventory of your own relationship to hospitality. Can you choose to make a natural, cheerful spirit of welcoming a normal part of your life?

Conversely, another way to honor Celtic hospitality is to learn how to be a humble yet grateful *recipient* of the generosity of others. When my daughter was sick and required daily care, my wife and I learned to rely not only on "official" help provided by our insurance company and social security, but also to receive the generous support of family, friends, and even strangers who simply wanted to help. Because we had been brought up to be self-sufficient and not wanting to impose on others, it was a learning experience for both of us to accept, with humility and grace, the blessings that others so freely gave us. But we realized that if we didn't accept others' generosity, not only were we at risk of burning out, but also we denied the others the chance to give.

When it comes to making hospitality a regular part of our lives, perhaps two principles apply here: letting things be imperfect and letting miracles unfold slowly. In other words, be hospitable toward yourself as you seek ways to cultivate hospitality in your world. No one needs to go from being Bres the Fomorian to becoming Mother Teresa overnight, but we all can find small ways to offer grace to others. Drive a little less aggressively. Invite the neighbors over for dinner. Take time to comfort an upset coworker. Visit your great aunt in the nursing home, and take her to church. And, of course, be available to host guests in your home—if not total strangers, then at least out-of-town friends when they're passing through. Remember, hospitality doesn't demand that your house feel like a five-star hotel. It just needs to be warm, clean, and most of all, loving.

Chapter Fourteen

Anamchara

One of the loveliest aspects of Celtic spirituality is the *anamchara* (also spelled *anam ċara*), a Gaelic word that means "soul friend." Apparently, this kind of relationship, combining the familiarity of friendship with the intimacy of caring for another person's soul or spirit, goes back to the druids themselves and was warmly embraced by Celtic Christians. Legend holds that Saint Brigid herself once said, "Anyone without a soul friend is like a body without a head." That seems to be a rather bold statement, but it reveals just how important this kind of relationship is to those who walk the Celtic path. So what makes someone a soul friend?

To begin with, it's an ordinary and down-to-earth role. A soul friend is someone with whom you might share the most intimate details of your spiritual journey. It's not a professional helper, like a therapist or a social worker. Although, especially in some forms of Christianity, there is a ministry called "spiritual direction" where individuals provide mentoring and support to others, soul friendship implies something even more humble and earthy. It's not some sort of luxury that bored socialites can indulge in between their garden club meetings. Rather, having a true friend of your soul is essential for allowing an authentic spiritual life to thrive within you. The ancients realized that truly engaging with the demands of the inner life meant being able to share the dynamics of your world with a trusted companion. Why would it be any different for us today?

Many of us rely on spiritual directors, meditation teachers, or others in formal positions of leadership to provide our "soul friend" experience. Some of us are fortunate enough to have someone in our lives who functions as an *anamchara* simply because this person has a natural affinity to this kind of amiable spiritual intimacy. But I'm afraid that far too many people feel as though they have no one to support them in their quest to nurture their souls. That's a sad situation, and perhaps the wisdom of the Celts can help all of us learn how to be better soul friends to each other.

Perhaps we need to make it a priority to be intentional about forming (or finding) at least one relationship that extends beyond just talking about the weather or the news or the daily drama of our feelings—and take the contemplative time necessary to truly befriend the hidden depths that lie within each of us, depths that we so rarely allow a voice.

What does a soul friend do? It's not a therapeutic relationship, so there's no agenda based on achieving a goal or managing an emotional or mental dysfunction. Nor is it a pastoral relationship, where a mentor provides theological and moral guidance to an apprentice. The soul friend is a spiritual companion—sort of like the best friend we turned to for advice and insight when we first fell in love as teenagers. It's not the job of a friend like this to provide answers or to fix problems—but rather simply to be present, to offer an opinion when it's appropriate to do so, but just as often to refrain from spewing unneeded advice.

The ideal soul friend is one who takes his or her own spiritual life seriously enough that there can be a shared language or vocabulary when discussing the landscape of the inner journey. Often a soul friend will share your religious or spiritual persuasion, but even this is not absolutely essential. Far better that your soul friend shares the yearning of your heart rather than the duties of your faith. In Christian terms, a soul friend will be your companion in prayer. Others might prefer to see such a person as a partner in meditation or even magic. Use the language that works for you—listen to your heart, and seek someone who speaks to it.

Who can be a soul friend? Almost anyone, really. I've heard it said that a husband or wife or lover is not the best choice, but that shouldn't be an inflexible rule—even though there's wisdom in befriending a person with a bit of distance. As I've already acknowledged, a minister or counselor can do the job, but that makes for a blurring of roles that might not always work out very well. Ideally, a soul friend is just exactly that—a friend who knows the soul (both his or her own, and yours). Someone with whom the most natural and appropriate style of relating is friendly—equal, relaxed, intimate without being sexually charged. Like all friends, this is a person with whom it's easy to feel you're "on the same side." The soul aspect has to do with the indefinable quality of interior depth and awareness that reaches out from your friend's inner landscape to your own and back again. That quality cannot be adequately described in a book. It can only be yearned for, searched for, and ultimately experienced. A soul friend cannot just be ordered through a website or found in a phonebook. A true *anamchara* may take weeks, months, even years to find. But such a connection is worth the wait—and the search.

What is it like to spend time with a soul friend? Well, that's up to you and your *anamchara*, isn't it? Some such friends may enjoy praying or meditating or creating art together, or sharing ideas and discussing interesting books you're both reading. Such friends may be the active sort who love to go hiking or the contemplative sort who prefer long moments of silence while the tea is brewing. Although some soul friends might spend nearly all their time talking about "spiritual stuff" and others bring it up only occasionally, there will be on some level a conscious sense of shared spirituality. But this can take many forms.

Likewise, soul friends might be very structured in their relationship, meeting for ninety minutes once a month, with a new appointment set up before the old one is finished. But it might just as easily be the sort of comfortable companionship that connects on a strictly "as-needed" basis. Conceivably, soul friends might live in the same building or on the other side of the world (thus communicating by mail, phone, or computer). If there's a shared religious orientation, presumably friends will enjoy the opportunity to do the work of their faith as part of their companionship, whether that means going to church together, participating in a service-oriented project, or reciting a shared prayer or sacred poem.

Like any friendship, part of the beauty here is how informal and relaxed the relationship can be. Intimacy, rather than institutionalization, is the driving force.

The paradox of a soul friend lies in this: to be a true soul friend, one should have a sense that this is what's going on. As I've said before, while most of us have or have had "accidental" soul friends, the true riches of this kind of relationship reveal themselves only when it is entered into consciously. And yet, the biggest threat to the soul friend connection (aside from our culture's hell-bent desire to turn spirituality into just another consumer commodity, which could threaten to turn soul friendship into a fashionable "must-have" spiritual accessory) is self-consciousness.

So one key to making this relationship work is humility, in the best sense of the word: that is to say, self-forgetfulness. I know I'm a friend of your soul, and so now I forget all about it—it's no big deal, really (and yet, it *is* a sacred big deal). This is a paradox, and we can only talk about it in oblique and mysterious ways. Yet it's a paradox worth keeping in mind. We need to value soul friendship enough to make it a priority—and then, having found a soul friend, we need to value the uniqueness and potential of the relationship itself by making it as unstructured and unbeholden to an agenda as possible.

Soul friends are accountable to one another. No, not in any sort of formalized way—it's not about keeping score. But good soul friends will be interested in how it goes with the deep and hidden places within each other. So it is natural for *anamchairde* to talk about declarations they've made about how they want their spiritual lives to grow, promises offered to God or each other or others, and a willingness to reflect together on where the integrity (and where the malarkey) can be found in each of their lives.

Spirituality sometimes can collapse into narcissism, if we aren't careful. We can get all cozy and comfy with our meditation or our prayer practice, cocooning with God or the angels or whomever else we allow into our precious inner universes. Soul friendship breathes space and light into that tightly bound dynamic, allowing the spiritual feedback loop to be integrated into the eyes and ears and discerning mind of at least one other soul.

What makes a soul friend relationship "Celtic"? Sure, the word *anamchara* is Gaelic enough, but the value and quality of a soul friendship are universal; this type of friendship can provide meaning in any cultural, religious, or spiritual context. This is something good to keep in mind. Celtic wisdom and spirituality are ultimately only valuable insofar as they help us not to be more purely or securely "Celtic," but rather provide insight and guidance into finding greater depth, joy, and connection in being *human*. Still, the soul friend comes to us specifically from the Celtic world, so it's fair to ask how Celtic symbolism and ideas shape this meaningful relationship.

I think the key lies in the qualities we have seen among the saints: hospitality, earthiness, honor, courage, and peacemaking. These are the characteristics that shape a deep friendship with a conscious spiritual dimension. Yes, you could argue that these are not just Celtic values; they are universal values. Yet it is in the context of the Celtic tradition that this particular way of understanding spiritual intimacy comes down to us, from both the druids and the early Celtic Christians. So here we have a lovely example of Celtic spirituality inspiring us simply to be more truly alive, more deeply connected with wisdom—in whatever form it might take.

An *anamchara* relationship embodies three of the most ancient of Celtic archetypes: the druid, the bard or storyteller, and the seer or visionary.

Like a druid, a soul friend can help us create rituals and ceremonies, or ask challenging questions, or learn powerful insights from psychology or science or history—in short, to help us to stay alert and mindful of our soul's needs. Like a bard, a soul friend can tell us meaningful stories and invite us to become the bard of the most important story we'll ever know—the unique and powerful story of our own soul's journey. And like a seer, a soul friend takes us beyond the dance of psychology into the ineffable realm of spiritual mystery and meaning, discovering the holy places within our hearts and souls, and traversing those gateways to encounter the eternal places that shape who we truly are.

Perhaps not every soul friend will do all of these things, or some friendships may be more druidic or more bardic in their orientation than others. That's okay. Remember—the *anamchara* is a gentle, ordinary, okay-to-be-imperfect kind of friend. And within that earthiness and simplicity, there's plenty of room for miracles to occur.

If you already have someone who is your soul friend (and you are his or hers), then cherish—and nurture—that bond. If not, perhaps put it in your prayers that such an intimate connection might become part of the symphony of your life, when the time is right, of course. Be patient, but be proactive about seeking a friend with whom you can share your soul. It is a relationship worth nurturing.

Chapter Fifteen

Shanachie

The first time I went to Ireland I spent a lovely day with a *shanachie.*

His name was Tom, and he lived on a farm in County Galway, near the town of Gort (where Lady Gregory lived and William Butler Yeats had a summer home). A fellow writer introduced me to him, saying that Tom was the world's foremost authority on the Celtic saint Colman—and since I'm a "son of Colman," it only made sense for Tom and me to meet. I had a busy schedule (I was in Ireland doing research for a book), but I'm sure glad I made time for old farmer Tom. He was retired, living with his wife in their modest farmhouse. All three children had moved to America, and he sorrowfully noted that none of them were interested in taking over the family farm. But his life was full of love and stories and poetry and song.

Tom met me at the Lady Gregory Inn, on a day when it so happened that Ireland was playing Spain for the World Cup. So the pub at the inn was filled with patriotic sports fans who wanted to see the game on the large-screen TVs in the company of their friends and neighbors. They were a noisy and rowdy bunch, but Tom and I managed to find a quiet corner where I had a Guinness and he had tea, and we sat for a good long chat.

No sooner had I mentioned that I was interested in the Irish storytelling tradition—for a *shanachie* is simply that, a traditional storyteller—than Tom began by telling a tale about the fairies. "The fairies are angels," he began, "not the bad angels who were sentenced to eternity in hell, nor the good angels who rallied behind Saint Michael when Lucifer revolted. No, the fairies were the neutral angels, and God sent them to the earth where they must wait until Judgment Day just like us humans." He went on to recount a never-ending stream of tales, some short enough that they barely took a minute, others considerably longer—stories about the fairies or about the saints or about local legends and lore. A couple of the tales I recognized from my own reading on Irish mythology and folklore, but most of them were unfamiliar to me, so I had no idea whether these were stories he had learned years ago, read out of a book, or embellished with his own way of seeing the world. And soon I realized that it didn't really matter.

Storytelling, as an art form, has long been a central way by which Celtic wisdom is transmitted. Closely related to the telling of stories is the recitation of poetry, and in the days before the coming of Christianity, Ireland and other Celtic lands gave rise to bards, professional poets/storytellers/mythmakers who were responsible for preserving the lore and history of their people. With the coming of Christianity, this role passed to the monks who laboriously documented the myths of old in written form— and wrote their own poetry as well, often humorous descriptions of their prayerful lives, and often shimmering with natural beauty. Over the centuries, the Celtic love of language, myth, poetry, story, and song continued to grow and evolve. In the late nineteenth and early twentieth centuries, folklorists like Alexander Carmichael in Scotland and Douglas Hyde in Ireland preserved the rich oral tradition of prayers, runes, charms, and songs that common people in the Gaelic-speaking lands recited day in and day out, to give shape to their faith and to express the depths of their spiritual wisdom. (Several of these poems, from Carmichael's anthology called *Carmina Gadelica*, are included in this book.)

Where else but in Ireland is there a famous stone that, it is said, grants the gift of eloquence to those who kiss it?

Of course, no discussion of the Celtic gift of storytelling would be complete without acknowledging the many great writers of Celtic ancestry—not all of whom are explicitly spiritual or religious. From James Joyce to Oscar Wilde, William Blake to William Butler Yeats, George MacDonald to C. S. Lewis, Kate O'Brien to Iris Murdoch, Seamus Heaney to John O'Donohue —our world is so much the richer for the "bards" over the centuries whose stories, poems, and words of inspiration continue to fill our imaginations with light and our hearts with longing.

In Celtic poetry and story and song, we hear the keening of the banshee's wail, lamenting the sorrows that accompany the human experience. We discover luminous worlds filled with wonder, places of imagination where heaven's light dances within our own eyes. We laugh with the foibles of the fairies, are inspired by the sacrifice of the saints, and remember what it means to be human in a world where nature itself is both a gift and our fostering mother. In short, Celtic spirituality is a spirituality that we encounter not through learned philosophy and theology, but through the whisper of the wind, the lyrics of a ballad, the rhymes of a poem, or the irony of a well-told joke.

How, then, do we "practice" the spirituality of Celtic stories? How do we weave stories and poetry into our own lives?

The first step may seem obvious enough, and that is to simply feast on the literature of the Celtic world as much and as often as you can. We are blessed to have the writings of so many great poets, novelists, playwrights, and spiritual teachers available to us in our time. Find a good collection of Irish or Welsh myths, and follow it up with anthologies of folk-lore or fairy tales from various parts of the Celtic world. You may be surprised at the wealth of writers who live in or hail from Celtic lands: a partial list would include Jonathan Swift, Oliver Goldsmith, Samuel Beckett, John Millington Synge, George Bernard Shaw, Katharine Tynan, Lady Gregory, Flann O'Brien, Dylan Thomas, Angharad Tomos, Gwyneth Lewis, Grace Coddington, Robert Burns, Irvine Welsh, Janice Galloway, Kenneth Grahame, R. S. Thomas, Jackie Kay, and Eavan Boland. For that matter, consider the great musicians of our time who have Celtic ancestry, including Van Morrison, Bono of U2, Annie Lennox of Eurythmics, and the late Dolores O'Riordan of The Cranberries.

If your interests run primarily along the lines of spiritual or inspirational writing, begin with some of the writers I've quoted or mentioned in this book, including C. S. Lewis, Seán Ó Duinn, and John O'Donohue. A few others worth exploring include John Philip Newell, Bernadette Flanagan, Mary Low, Ray Simpson, Kenneth McIntosh, Gareth Higgins, and David Cole. And that's just the tip of the Celtic iceberg.

But there's more to making Celtic stories and poems part of your life than just enjoying the words of others, as delightful as that might be. Part of the beauty of traditional Celtic spirituality is how nonhierarchical it was: at a traditional *ceilidh*—a festive gathering where neighbors come together for music, dancing, and conviviality—everyone was encouraged to have a song to sing, a story to tell, or a poem to recite. What made it magic was not having one or two people who did all the performing while everyone else simply formed an audience. Rather, the beauty of sharing stories and songs arose precisely in how inclusive such an event could be. Sooner or later, it's your turn to share your story.

If you are an introvert, or simply lack confidence in your own creative abilities, sharing your story might seem daunting. But not everyone is called to be as eloquent as Yeats, as nimble as Michael Flatley, or as funny as Billy Connolly. What matters is that you find *your* voice. Tell *your* story, or write *your* poems. If you're too shy to share them with others, well, keep a journal and share them only with God. But the important thing is to write, to keep that journal, to tell your story, whether you do so in poetry, prose, song, or even fiction.

Why does this matter? Consider the great spiritual traditions of not just the Celtic lands, but the world over. From Buddhism to Daoism to Judaism to Islam to Christianity, spiritual wisdom has been transmitted from generation to generation through the written word. Meanwhile, keeping a journal as a way of becoming intentional about one's own unfolding spirituality is a universally recognized practice. Not only have some of the greatest spiritual teachers of all time begun writing by keeping journals (from Saint Augustine in the fourth century to Thomas Merton in the twentieth), but "ordinary" spiritual seekers also find that writing down our dreams, our prayers, our insights, and our ordinary miracles can be a powerful spiritual discipline all its own—and a wonderful record of one's spiritual journey that only grows more valuable over time.

Of course, if you feel inspired to walk in the footsteps of writers like George MacDonald or C. S. Lewis, and tell stories inspired by the rich mysticism of the Celtic world, with an eye to publication, that can be its own richly rewarding spiritual practice.

There's no one right way to tell your story—or any story. Likewise, there's no one right way to write (or recite) a poem. But when you wrestle with the beauty and mystery of language, seeking to find just the right way to express something that probably lies beyond the grasp of ordinary words anyway, you are stepping into a rich tradition of insight and prayer that extends all the way back to the saints and the bards. It's a beautiful tradition to be part of.

Chapter Sixteen

Neart

One key to unlocking the treasures of Celtic spirituality and wisdom lies in a simple Irish word: *neart*. In Old Irish *nert*, this word dances through the prayers and poems of Celtic saints and monks.

MacLennan's *Dictionary of the Gaelic Language* defines *neart* as "force, pith, power, might, energy, vigour; vast quantity; number, superabundance." But none of these definitions captures the essence of *neart*—it is more than the sum of its parts.

This wonderful word represents how a variety of spiritually meaningful concepts intersect within the Celtic heart and mind. *Neart* represents the life-energy of abundance. It signifies the strength of God's protection and the power of God to heal. It is the fundamental energy that flows at the heart of all things—an energy that not only keeps things going but also fills everything with potential and possibility. Christians might say it is the energy of Divine Love, or perhaps even a sign of the Holy Spirit's presence in our lives. If you prefer a more nontheistic approach, *neart* could symbolize something akin to the impersonal "Force" of *Star Wars* fame—except that there's no dualism within *neart*—no "light side" or "dark side." In the words of one of my favorite characters in contemporary children's books, Pete the Cat: "It's all good." *Neart* is the energy of Celtic nonduality: it holds all things together in its heart of power and prosperity.

In *Where Three Streams Meet*, Seán Ó Duinn suggests that *neart* could be thought of as *mana*, the Polynesian concept of "life-force." This brings to my mind a variety of other ways of thinking about *neart*: it is akin to *reiki*, the Japanese concept similar to *mana*—of "Universal Life-Force." It is *prana*—a similar concept found in the Sanskrit tradition. Sure, it's dangerous to draw sweeping parallels like this that blithely hop across cultures and their distinctive ways of understanding the cosmos—and yet, one of the treasures of *neart* is how it offers us both a sense of the energy that pulsates through all things *and* how that energy is a source of plenty. In this way of seeing things, *neart* may not be exactly the same as similar concepts from other cultures, but it is close enough to celebrate common ground. We can leave it to the scholars to split the hairs that separate *mana* from *neart*, and so forth. In the meantime, Celtic spirituality can join numerous other wisdom traditions in affirming that the world we live in is not a place of scarcity and hardship—at least not essentially. No matter what material challenges we face, we are all custodians of immense spiritual wealth.

So how does *neart* function in our ordinary lives? Let's begin with faith. Believing something can often be the first essential key to making it so. People who believe in the power of prayer are far more likely to report it making a real, observable difference in their lives. For those who don't believe, maybe it's just a matter of prayer not being given credit where it's due—or perhaps lack of faith can be an obstacle to the flow of energy (read: *neart*) in our lives. You want a miracle? Begin by believing it. No, not just paying it lip service, but choosing to live your life in a way that creates the amazing open-minded possibility that a four-alarm-way-too-big-to-be-a-coincidence miracle just might manifest for you. Sure, not every circumstance results in miracles: God is not in the habit of breaking God's own laws. But once in a while, it seems that the laws of nature do get bent, or slipped around. And it's *neart* that's doing the bending and slipping.

Choose to open your mind and heart and soul to the power and flow of *neart*. It's exciting to believe that, at any moment in time, at any place anywhere, something amazingly wonderful, entirely unexpected, and undeserved may possibly happen. With a belief like that, it's so much easier to live by hope, rather than to sink in cynicism and despair. Yeah, sure, the odds may be against a miracle—well, the odds are against winning the lottery, too, and how many of us pop a dollar (or five) across the counter at the gas station "just in case"? Opening our hearts to the magic of *neart* doesn't even cost us anything. When my father was alive, he used to buy lottery tickets—just one at a time. He used to say, "As soon as I buy that ticket, I just assume I'm a millionaire. And if I don't win, well, I'll just buy another ticket. Then I'm a millionaire all over again." My dad didn't live extravagantly—he was a stickler for paying the credit card off in full every month and understood that the secret to living well was living below one's means. But he did live by faith. And so the *neart* flowed through him, and even on his retirement pension, he felt like he was worth a million bucks.

Opening up to the flow of *neart* is a lot like faith in God. It's a decision, a choice, a commitment—but one that cultivates a heart that trusts and a mind that is open to unexpected blessings. It's saying "YES" to life, to love, to possibilities, to hope. It's deciding that it's a whole lot more fun, effective, and meaningful to live from a sense that the cosmos we inhabit is a safe place, a place that is good and nurturing and plentiful, than to shrink within a self-armoring idea that there's never enough, every one is out for himself or herself, ultimately there is no meaning. Sure, suffering is real—faith is not honest when it denies the shadow side of life. But when life kicks us in the teeth, it's so very tempting to become cynicism's slave. But where does that ultimately lead us? Only to an ever-yawning downward spiral of despair. It can be cool, hip, intellectual, ironic, fashionable to be the cynic, the skeptic, the professional doubter, but at the end of the day, it simply doesn't feel very good—and it doesn't lead us anywhere. Meanwhile, those of us who open our hearts to *neart* go through life expecting miracles at any moment. Go ahead, call us naïve or even Pollyannaish. But who's got the smile—the real smile, that goes way down deep inside?

Take faith in *neart* a step further. Once we choose to believe in a force for life and power and miracles, then we actually are capable of experiencing that creative flow through us. Maybe it's a physical sensation—similar to reiki, which can be experienced as a warmth or tingling sensation flowing through those who use the energy when doing healing-touch work with others. Or maybe it's not so much a feeling, but a telltale pattern of serendipity and blessings that flow through our lives and the lives of those we know and love. In other words, we can recognize it by the trail it leaves behind—a trail of happiness, of satisfaction, of a sense of Divine presence moving through the world. It creates a swath of joy, and anyone who believes that such a thing exists can start to see the evidence for it. A teacher of mine instructs her students to look for three miracles in their lives every day. Inevitably someone asks for a definition of "miracle." Must it be something supernatural? Well, not necessarily—"miracle" is related to "mirror" and refers to a reflection of Divine power in our lives; a reflection of *neart*. And that can come in small as well as huge ways. At least three times a day.

Celtic spirituality has a reputation for being optimistic. Certainly, Celtic Christianity is a remarkably positive expression of faith in Christ, and indigenous Celtic wisdom, with its emphasis on the beauty of nature, the nobility of the hero, and the immortality of the soul likewise shimmers with hope and trust. I like to think this upbeat characteristic of the Celtic path begins with the reality of *neart*. If we live in a universe pulsating with power and abundance, then ultimately our problems are solvable, surmountable—there's nothing to fear.

It's reminiscent of Jesus's overarching message: Be not afraid. So many of his followers are wracked with fear, fear of offending God, fear of damnation, fear that others will be lost just because they live or think differently. Optimism is a choice. It's the product of faith, for it requires a hopeful approach to life. Faith says, "I believe in the blessings of God; I trust in the flow of *neart*," while optimism says, "I'll experience its blessings most any day now." They go hand in hand for those seeking to live a life of spiritual wisdom.

Neart is more than just a psychological strategy for cultivating hope and faith and optimistic thinking. It's also a cause for living a life according to the dictates of those positive values. If you want water to flow through a pump, you have to prime it. If you want *neart* to flow through your life, you "prime the pump" by creating the space in your heart to trust in the blessings to come. That space is created through hospitality, friendship, and contemplation—good Celtic virtues, all. The only way for *neart* to flow *to* us is by creating the means for it to flow *through* us, which means finding ways to give it to others. Funny—the same thing is often said of love: the best way to find it is to give it away. It has been said that in heaven and hell, we have no elbows. Those who suffer in hell struggle with their inability to feed themselves, since an arm that won't bend cannot bring food up to the mouth. But in heaven, this same physical circumstance is no problem: for you see, everyone feeds someone else. *And no one gets left out.*

Neart, it seems to me, brings all the strands of Celtic wisdom together. *Rinnfheitheamh*—the edge of waiting—is, ultimately, waiting for the blessings of *neart* to flow in our lives. A Thin Place is a place where the pulsating presence of *neart* seems to flow especially strongly and well. The saints all embodied *neart* in their lives, and what is hospitality but the willingness to share *neart* with a stranger, just as two *anamchairde* or soul friends share *neart* with each other?

Call it the luck of the Irish—or just the evidence of God's love, call it energy, call it hope, call it a fuel of miracles. For those who choose to see, it's as plain as the nose on our face. *Neart* provides us with ready access to the energy of Divine Love, an energy that keeps us connected to blessings. The energy is more than just the bringer of blessing—it is blessing itself.

Chapter Seventeen

The Grail

A little book like this can give you only a taste of the treasures found in the heart of the Celtic soul. My goal in writing this brief book was not to speak the last word on Celtic wisdom (as if that were possible!). Rather, my hope is that you will catch a hint of the beauty and splendor of Celtic spirituality and initiate your own quest to drink deeply from the holy wells of Celtic wisdom.

It's rather like the quest for the Holy Grail.

King Arthur symbolizes many things. He is a face for the sovereignty of Celtic Britain, defending his island home against the encroaching Saxon barbarians who came after the departure of the Romans in the fifth century. He also embodies the ideals of chivalry, a code of conduct where honor, gentility, respect for those who lack power, and social refinement take precedence over the mere assertion of strength or will. As the central figure of a wide-ranging cycle of poetry and romance, Arthur symbolizes a literary world of pageantry, tournaments, and knighthood—but also palace intrigue, adultery, betrayal, and broken family relationships that carry tragic consequences. In short, Arthur is both an ideal of nobility and a deeply flawed, deeply human archetypal figure.

No one knows if King Arthur is purely a literary invention or if there really was a historical Arthur who defended Britain (at least for a time) against the barbarian invaders. But if Arthur did exist, then he most probably was a Celtic chieftain. The Celts were a tribal people, so the "high kings" that populate Irish mythology were probably little more than regional lords (if they existed at all). The same could be said of Arthur. But as I have said before, to try to unravel the complex knot where history, legend, mythology, and folklore all come together is ultimately to miss the point of Celtic wisdom.

For Arthur, that point is most fully realized not in the dashing tales of knights in shining armor, or even in the fragile system of governance that the Round Table symbolized. Rather, the heart of Celtic wisdom, as encoded in Arthurian legend, consists of the quest for the Holy Grail.

Thanks to our entertainment-besotted culture, many of us may associate the Holy Grail primarily with the adventures of Indiana Jones or the hijinks of Monty Python. But the quest for the Grail has Celtic roots that run deep—deeper even than the association with the cup Christ used at the last supper. Before Christianity, the "grail" may have been the cauldron of plenty, presided over by the Irish god of abundance, An Dagda. Others associate the grail in more general terms with the goddess, which parallels with the idea popular in some circles that the true "grail" was actually Mary Magdalene, a symbol of the divine feminine.

Rather than getting caught up on which theory makes the most sense, I think the grail needs to remain mysterious and elusive. Is it the container that holds the precious blood of Christ? The cauldron from which all blessings flow? The secret to the feminine face of the Divine? Or perhaps the grail simply represents a portal to enlightenment, which might mean something slightly different for each of us.

However you understand the grail, it is a treasure, lost or hidden, that beckons you to search for it. Even if you believe this treasure is hidden in plain sight, it remains hidden and you are called to find it, to reveal it, to point out where it has been all along.

So much has been left unsaid in this book. We haven't talked about *imbas*, the "fire in the head" or the inspiration that bubbles forth in all prayer and poetry. We haven't considered that loveliest of images for the Holy Spirit, the Wild Goose (much beloved by the Christians in the Iona Community), and all that it signifies: that the love of God is something wild, untamed, uncontrollable, always on the move, always present yet seemingly just beyond our grasp.

Perhaps chasing the Wild Goose is just another way of describing the quest for the grail.

The old Arthurian romances suggest that it was a knight's most noble calling to seek the grail, and that only the purest and noblest of knights could hope to attain the object of his quest. I'm not sure how "Celtic" that notion is, however. The Celts seem to be a people who understand that life is messy and complex, and that even the greatest of heroes has a flaw (or many)—Cúchulainn rejects the love of the goddess Morrigan, and it is she who engineers that fatal encounter with the old hag offering him the dog-meat soup. He may have been the greatest warrior Ireland has ever known, but he was flawed, and his flaw was his undoing. Saint Kevin, likewise, feared the feminine, and Columcille's pride (and willingness to copy a book without permission) led to the loss of many lives. Celtic wisdom does not require us to be perfect; on the other hand, it acknowledges that we most certainly are not.

But it has been said that God draws straight with crooked lines, and perhaps that's the deeper message of the imperfect characters who populate Celtic history, myth, and legend. This means that for imperfect people like you and me, the grail is not off-limits. We are invited onto the quest, despite our flaws, our brokenness, our woundedness, our sins. This is not to give us a free pass: we are still called to repentance, to clean up our messes whenever we make them, to do the hard work of healing and reconciliation. But the quest for the grail is not something separate from the messiness of living. On the contrary, it happens right in the middle of the mess.

So, my friends, here I must take my leave. Now I encourage you to explore the stories further as your own interest and inclinations direct you. Make time in your life to befriend the silence at the edge of waiting, and open your heart to the healing power of *neart*. Offer hospitality to soul friends and strangers, and learn to tell your own story. Even if you don't realize it now, you will find that your story is indeed *the* story: the quest for the grail, the chasing of the Wild Goose. See where it leads you. And look with wonder.

DHE, thug mis a fois na h-oidhch an raoir   O GOD, who brought me from the rest of last night
Chon solus aoibh an la an diugh,   Unto the joyous light of this day,
Bi da mo thoir bho sholus ur an la an diugh, Be Thou bringing me from the new light of this day
Chon solus iul na siorruidheachd,   Unto the guiding light of eternity.
    O! bho sholus ur an la an diugh,   Oh! from the new light of this day
    Gu solus iul na siorruidheachd.   Unto the guiding light of eternity.

—*Carmina Gadelica*

ACKNOWLEDGMENTS

Portions of this book first appeared in my book of daily Celtic meditations, *366 Celt: A Year and a Day of Celtic Wisdom and Lore*. Other bits and pieces first appeared on my blog. Some of the ideas and insights in this book arose from retreats and classes on Celtic spirituality that I taught in various settings, including Emory University Continuing Education, Columbia Theological Seminary's Center for Lifelong Learning, Charlotte Spirituality Center, Montreat Conference Center, St. Patrick's Episcopal Church (Dunwoody, Georgia), and the Cerveny Conference Center of the Episcopal Diocese of North Florida. Special thanks to the students and retreatants who participated in these programs; your questions and comments helped immensely in developing this material.

Many thanks to Greg Brandenburgh and Linda Roghaar and everyone at Hampton Roads/Red Wheel Weiser for your parts in making this book a reality.

Over the years a variety of folks who share my love for Celtic spirituality and wisdom have offered me guidance, inspiration, mentoring, soul friendship, and/or great conversations over a pint. Some of these luminous souls and soul friends include Linda Abel, David Cole, Cait Finnegan, Andrew Fitz-Gibbon, Gareth Higgins, Kenneth McIntosh, and Kurt Neilson. I suspect I'm leaving out somebody I dearly love: such is the curse of an aging brain. If you are that person, please forgive my distracted mind. I'll pay you back in the next world.

The prayer-poems scattered throughout this book come from *Carmina Gadelica* (the "charms of the Gaels"), an anthology of traditional oral religious hymns, incantations, runes, blessings, and supplications collected by the Scottish folklorist Alexander Carmichael. The first two volumes of this six-volume compendium of Celtic Christian wisdom can be found online at *www.sacred-texts.com/neu /celt/cg.htm.*

Finally, I should mention my literary and spiritual debt to John O'Donohue, whom I met only once (although we had a lovely couple of hours together while I interviewed him for an article I was writing; a transcript of the interview appears on my blog). John's lyrical sense of Celtic spirituality transcended a mere appreciation of the poetry of history (beautiful though that may be) to truly embody how the wisdom of Celtic consciousness makes a real difference in the most ordinary and down-to-earth dimensions of life and living. John left us far too soon, but thankfully his poetry and poetic prose continue to nurture us and will inspire generations to come.

ABOUT THE AUTHOR

Carl McColman is the author of *The Big Book of Christian Mysticism*, *The Little Book of Christian Mysticism*, *Christian Mystics*, and *Answering the Contemplative Call*, along with a popular website and blog devoted to Christian and world mystical spirituality (*www.carlmccolman.com*). He regularly speaks and leads retreats on various aspects of the spiritual life, including the mysteries of Celtic wisdom. Carl lives near Atlanta, Georgia.

Ingram Content Group UK Ltd.
Milton Keynes UK
UKHW010732280323
419285UK00006B/474

9 781506 485249